HOW DO EXPERT PRIMARY CLASSTEACHERS REALLY WORK?

A critical guide for teachers, headteachers and teacher educators

Critical Guides for
Teacher Educators

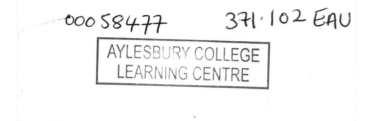
First published in 2012 by Critical Publishing Limited

British Library Cataloguing in Publication Data
A CIP record for this book is available from the British Library

ISBN: 978-1-909330-01-6

This book is also available in the following e-book formats:
Kindle ISBN: 978-1-909330-02-3
EPUB ISBN: 978-1-909330-03-0
Adobe e-book ISBN: 978-1-909330-04-7

The right of Tony Eaude to be identified as the Author of this work
has been asserted by him in accordance with the Copyright,
Design and Patents Act 1988.

Cover and text design by Greensplash Limited
Project Management by Out of House Publishing
Printed and bound in Great Britain by TJ International

Critical Publishing
www.criticalpublishing.com

MIX
Paper from
responsible sources
FSC® C013056

HOW DO **EXPERT** PRIMARY **CLASSTEACHERS** REALLY WORK?

A critical guide for teachers, headteachers and teacher educators

Critical Guides for
Teacher Educators

Tony Eaude

CONTENTS

ABOUT THE **AUTHOR**

Dr Tony Eaude was previously a headteacher of a multicultural primary school in Oxford. After studying for a doctorate at the Department of Education, University of Oxford, he has worked independently, mainly in research evaluation, writing and teaching both adults and children. His publications reflect his interest in children's learning and how this can best be enhanced, and he is passionate about the need to change current approaches to teaching young children. More details of his work can be found on www.edperspectives.org.uk.

Acknowledgements

I should like to thank those people involved in Higher Education who have pointed me, both through their writing and in person, towards the different traditions of research on which this book draws. I wish to acknowledge the contribution of many thoughtful and dedicated primary classteachers with a high level of expertise with whom I have worked, though most of them were modest, and often uncertain, about this and what it entailed. I am grateful to Julia Morris at Critical Publishing, and her colleagues, for their expertise in producing the book so quickly. In particular, I wish to thank Jude Egan for her encouragement, support and love, especially when I was unsure whether the questions explored in this book were the right ones to ask. I hope that readers will think that they are and be encouraged to consider both on their own and with colleagues the implications for how teachers can best enhance young children's learning.

CHAPTER 1| INTRODUCTION

> *The regular classroom teacher is confronted, not with a single patient, but with a classroom filled with 25 to 35 youngsters. The teacher's goals are multiple ... Even in the ubiquitous primary reading group, the teacher must simultaneously be concerned with the learning of decoding skills as well as comprehension, with motivation and love of reading as well as word-attack, and must monitor the performance of the six to eight students in front of her while not losing touch with the other two dozen in the room ... The only time a physician could possibly encounter a situation of comparable complexity would be in the emergency room of a hospital during or after a natural disaster.*
>
> (Shulman, 2004, p 504)

Setting the scene

I wonder how you respond to this quotation. Do you see the role of a primary classteacher as comparable to that of a doctor? Or a lawyer? Or a scientist? Most people would think that teaching a class of young children is far easier, as reflected in status and salary. This book argues that Shulman is right and explores why.

This is not a manual of how to teach reading, or science, or art, but an exploration of how classteachers with a high level of expertise with young children really work and the challenges they face. It is based on three core beliefs, that:

> » as Fullan (1991, p 117) writes, *educational change depends on what teachers do and think. It's as simple and complex as that;*
>
> » teaching young children is profoundly important and complicated, but poorly understood; and
>
> » ideas related to expertise are helpful in understanding how this is done well and encouraging classteachers to think more deeply about their work.

This book is therefore written to encourage teachers, headteachers and teacher educators, and others outside the profession, to think critically about how classteachers can enhance young children's learning and their lives; and to help raise the status of those who teach them.

Long regarded patronisingly as women's work, and often linked more to care than education, teaching young children was long seen as not requiring much training, qualification or intellect – or certainly not as much as teaching older children. In case you think that this attitude has disappeared, you need only recall the idea of 'Mum's army' in the early 1990s or look at the pay structure where those teaching the youngest children earn least. Stories of those moving to teach younger children being asked why they have been demoted are still common.

This book presents a very different view and challenges many widely held assumptions. These, and the language in which they are framed, shape how we have come to think about teaching and learning. For instance, an emphasis on 'what works' and 'effectiveness', however seductive, fails to recognise that these make sense only in reference to what one seeks to achieve; and that the aims of education are multiple and, at times, contradictory. To see teaching as reducible to a series of competences underplays the extent to which expertise consists of subtle and interlinked features, hard to assess on the observation of one lesson, or even a few. The language of 'delivery' implies a view of knowledge as factual, like a box of groceries, and of teaching as mainly involving transmission. All of these assumptions should, I believe, be questioned.

Compliance and prescription

My interest in teacher expertise stems from my own experience as a teacher, a headteacher and someone involved in leading professional development for teachers and students. I became concerned about how children in primary schools were being taught and how their teachers approached and understood their role. This involves what the Cambridge Primary Review (Alexander, 2010) has called a culture of compliance, where teachers are told how to teach and children expected to conform.

Most teachers in primary schools have come to accept being told (often by those with little knowledge or recent experience of teaching young children) how to teach, with a prescribed model based on simple and largely non-negotiable guidance, with a strong emphasis on content and outcomes in literacy and numeracy. Ofsted inspection teams and the new Teachers' Standards (DfE, 2012) tend to see 'outstanding' teaching as based on 'what works' in raising scores in literacy and numeracy, without distinguishing how individuals may work in different ways, depending on the age of the children, the context and the objectives to be met. In contrast, this book suggests that teachers should constantly reflect on these for themselves and with other colleagues, to make judgements about how to teach, based on practical and theoretical knowledge and experience.

Teachers' suspicion of pedagogy

As the Cambridge Primary Review (Alexander, 2010, p 55) argues, *teachers should work towards a pedagogy of repertoire rather than recipe and of principle rather than prescription.* This involves teachers exercising choice and judgement based on a wide and deep knowledge both of learning and teaching, constantly developing this and not being inhibited from doing so. Without this, it is hard to see how teaching can claim a status comparable to other professions.

No one would consult a doctor who did not keep up with medical research, or go to a lawyer who ignored recent judgements. And it would cause an outcry if the government prescribed how a doctor conducted an operation. Yet, such an approach seems acceptable in teaching. This appears to be linked to teachers' suspicion of theory and research – and to being so busy that there is little time for reading and reflection. This leaves the profession open to the view that 'anyone can teach' and makes it harder for teachers to argue for 'a high level of autonomy' and to provide a rationale for practices which will 'prioritise the client's welfare', two characteristics of professionalism which John (2008, p 12) identifies.

Teachers, especially in primary schools, have always found it hard and been reluctant to articulate what constitutes good practice, especially in teaching a class over a whole year, and to engage with the detail of pedagogy. This is reflected in the titles of Simon's article 'Why No Pedagogy?' (1981) and Alexander's 'Still Why No Pedagogy?' (2004). Yet *mastery of a knowledge base requiring a long period of training* is another characteristic of a profession identified by John (2008, p 12). Teachers' distrust of the term 'pedagogy' was illustrated by the comment of an experienced ex-colleague (and friend) who said that she would not read my book, *Thinking through Pedagogy for Primary and Early Years* (Eaude, 2011), as she had always avoided any reference to pedagogy.

The Cambridge Primary Review (Alexander, 2010, p 280) provides a useful definition of pedagogy as:

the act of teaching together with its attendant discourse of educational theories, values, evidence and justifications. It is what one needs to know, and the skills one needs to command, in order to make and justify the many different kinds of decision of which teaching is constituted.

This frame of reference, which does not equate teaching with instruction has, as the Review continues, been taken for granted for centuries in other countries, but not in England. The stronger traditions of pedagogy in systems such as those in Germany and the Scandinavian countries have provided a greater degree of assurance among teachers of how to teach; and with it some protection from the demands of politicians to teach in particular ways.

Teacher expertise

I was introduced to the extensive literature, mostly from the USA, on expertise and teacher expertise, which provides the basis for this book, by reading chapter 21 of the Cambridge Primary Review (Alexander, 2010, pp 406–36). You may be uneasy, as I am, with the idea of a teacher 'being an expert', and not just because of the self-deprecation characteristic of most of those who teach young children. The Cambridge Primary Review (Alexander, 2010, p 416) cites research which characterises five different stages of the development of expertise, on a continuum from novice, to advanced beginner, to competent, to proficient and to expert. But the idea of 'novices' and 'experts' in an activity as complex as teaching does not feel quite right to me. It is unlikely that someone will teach geography and maths equally well to the same group of ten year-olds or will have the same level of expertise with nine year-olds as with five year-olds, or that those in an affluent area will operate as successfully in an inner-city school – or vice versa. Any teacher's expertise will differ according to subject area, context and the children's background and culture. This leads me to talk of teachers with a high level of expertise rather than expert teachers, as such. However, when not specifically discussing teachers, I tend to stick to the term 'experts'.

Another significant influence in writing this book has been the Teaching and Learning Research Project (TLRP), a large-scale, cross-phase project, which suggested three fundamental changes of thinking, applicable to learners of all ages (TLRP, 2006). These are that:

> *learning processes, as distinct from learning contexts, do not fundamentally change as children become adults* and that pedagogy *has the advantage of highlighting the contingent nature of effective teaching i.e. the interventions of teachers or trainers are most effective when they are planned in response to how learners are learning;*

> *the conception of what is to be learned needs to be broadened beyond the notions of curricula and subjects associated with schools*; and

> *more prominence needs to be given to the importance of learning relationships.*

I shall suggest that all three are especially important in teaching young children. However, neither the TLRP nor Pollard (2010), which draws on its work thoughtfully and succinctly, address what is distinctive about particular phases. This book tries to open up discussion on the challenges of teaching a class of young children, drawing on research on:

> expertise in general and teacher expertise in particular; and

> young children's learning and development from infancy upwards, emphasising the social and emotional aspects of learning and the personal and interpersonal aspects of teaching.

This is in the belief that these provide a sounder basis for understanding learning and teaching since the underlying patterns of learning and behaviour are established in the early years of life; and that teachers have to take account of such influences in how they teach.

The structure of this book

This book tries to summarise key features of a large, often-contested, body of academic research to explore how classteachers with a high level of expertise with young children really work – not when putting on a special display, or in one particular lesson, but in working day to day with a class, over time.

In some respects, the task is impossible because no two individuals act in the same way. That is how professionals work in unpredictable situations. However, to try to identify common features is necessary if we are to understand, or at least explore, the complexity and subtlety of the classteacher's role. For reasons discussed in Chapters 2 and 3, this discussion is descriptive rather than prescriptive – in other words, it indicates broad features of how teachers with a high level of expertise work, rather than prescribing how any one teacher should.

Chapter 2 considers the nature of expertise in general and Chapter 3 teacher expertise more specifically. This indicates that teacher expertise is:

» prototypical, that is within broad, fluid boundaries to take account of individual difference;

» situated, that is specific to the learning needs of a particular age group or context; and

» mostly tacit and so hard for either the teacher or an observer to describe, however easily recognised.

This provides the rationale for the rest of the book in that the search for one model or style of teaching applicable to all situations is both unfruitful and a distraction. Rather one must recognise the challenges and opportunities of both the national and local policy context and, most crucially, the learning needs of children of a particular age and the specific class.

Children up to the age of 11 spend much of their time in school with one teacher and, broadly speaking, the same class group. Chapter 4, therefore, considers the role of the primary classteacher, recognising the complex dynamics of a class of young children and the pressure of external expectations. This leads into the discussion in Chapter 5 of how classteachers with a high level of expertise enhance young children's learning. These two chapters are intended to provoke thought and debate, rather than be the last word. Chapter 6 compares teachers with a high level of expertise with others and sketches out some implications for the development of teacher expertise. Each of the four main chapters starts with critical issues to be addressed and three end by making a key point in relation to each critical issue, after a brief summary of the main argument, 'in a nutshell'. The exception is Chapter 5, which ends by suggesting 12 propositions about primary classteachers with a high level of expertise.

While many of the ideas will be unfamiliar and may be hard-going, I have tried to use simple and accessible language and include illustrative examples, but I do not present easy answers, not least because one should be wary of such answers. Rather, I suggest ideas, challenges and dilemmas, recognising that teaching, especially a class of young children, is complex. So, at times, I ask the reader to think of other examples and I suggest that you do stop occasionally to reflect on the ideas presented. While much of my focus is on children between seven and 11, I am only rarely specific about age, since children are on a continuum of development and their learning is influenced by many others factors including prior experience, familiarity with the subject and motivation.

IN A **NUTSHELL**

This book presents teaching a class of young children as a very complex task, comparable to that of a doctor. Understanding this requires several deeply rooted assumptions about children's learning, about the qualities and the knowledge necessary to teach them well and about the current structures and approaches to schools to be challenged. It is designed to prompt thinking and debate rather than provide definitive answers, with the main questions addressed in each chapter set out in the box below. So, I hope you will be prepared to question, challenge and reflect and see how this fits with your own experience – and that this book will make you see the role differently.

CRITICAL ISSUES **TO BE ADDRESSED**

- *What does the research on expertise, in any field, indicate? (Chapter 2)*
- *What can we learn from the research on teacher expertise? (Chapter 3)*
- *What is distinctive about the role of the primary classteacher? (Chapter 4)*
- *How do primary classteachers with a high level of expertise work and think? (Chapter 5)*
- *What distinguishes teachers with a high level of expertise from others and how is expertise developed? (Chapter 6)*

CRITICAL **ISSUES**

- *How do experts (in any field) actually operate?*
- *Do all experts in the same field work in the same way?*
- *To what extent is expertise specific to a particular activity?*
- *How do we identify the features of expertise in ourselves or other people?*
- *In which respects can teachers learn from other professions?*
- *How is expertise developed?*

Introduction

Many years ago, I attended a course to become a hockey coach. The international goalkeeper visited and was asked to explain a difficult skill, using the stick to dispossess an oncoming forward. Although not properly equipped, he agreed to demonstrate. We watched as he took the ball, from a good player, apparently without effort. Asked to repeat it, he did so. It was only then, with questions related to aspects such as body position, balance and timing, that we watchers – and I suspect he – could identify key coaching points.

This story illustrates that complex tasks often look simple and effortless when carried out by an expert, but are difficult for someone less expert to do or even to describe in detail. The goalkeeper's knowledge was what Polanyi (1967) calls 'tacit', which neither he nor the watchers found easy to articulate. Whatever the expertise – as trampolinist, taxi driver or teacher – and whether as an observer or as the expert practitioner, expertise is easily recognised but only described with difficulty.

This chapter considers expertise in general, whether that of chess players or nuclear physicists, engineers or therapists, before looking, in Chapter 3, at teacher expertise more specifically. However, we should first recognise three difficulties.

Difficulties with the term expertise

1. Berliner (2001, pp 464–68) discusses two major challenges in researching expertise. The first is the role of talent – to what extent expertise is a question of innate ability, environmental factors and practice. This is especially pertinent in activities like music and sport. However, he concludes that this is *of little*

practical interest to those who study pedagogical expertise (p 465), suggesting that *it is probably the power of context followed by deliberate practice, more than talent, which influences a teacher's level of competency* (p 466).

2.   A second, more serious, difficulty is the lack of objective criteria in many fields for what constitutes expertise. In some, such as bridge or ice skating, results are clear indicators of this. However, in most, *one is usually deemed to be an expert by the judgement of others* (Berliner 2001, p 466), with this often being heavily influenced by cultural norms. In other words, the level of expertise demonstrated by the same person or performance may be judged differently by a range of observers.

3.   The third difficulty follows from this and the tacit nature of expertise. This is that expertise is not just manifested in results, or even in particular behaviours. Rather it is shown in how experts act and think about what they do, not just in one episode, but over a period of time, especially in complex social situations with a range of aims and outcomes, such as teaching. Berliner (2001, p 466) highlights that expertise is not just a characteristic of the person, but of the interaction of the person and the environment in which they work. So, the context affects how the expert can, and does, act, and what works in one context may not be effective in another. One obvious example is where there is a lack of resources, so that a science experiment, or a musical performance, may have to be adapted, or even abandoned, if equipment is missing or extraneous noise interferes. Less obvious examples are that different cultural traditions and expectations or external demands, such as the requirements for immediate results, affect how, and how well, an expert operates.

We return to these in relation to teaching in Chapter 3.

What the research suggests about expertise in general

Berliner (2001, pp 463–64) summarises a series of propositions about expertise which Glaser (1999) believes to be defensible. Slightly shortened, these are that:

» expertise is specific to a domain, developed over hundreds and thousands of hours, and continues to develop;

» development of expertise is not linear, with plateaus occurring, indicating shifts of understanding;

» expert knowledge is structured better for use in performance than is novice knowledge;

» experts represent problems in qualitatively different – deeper and richer – ways than novices;

>> experts recognise meaningful patterns faster than novices;

>> experts are more flexible and more opportunistic planners and can change representations faster, when appropriate, than novices;

>> experts impose meaning on, and are less easily misled by, ambiguous stimuli;

>> experts may start to solve a problem slower than a novice but overall they are faster problem solvers;

>> experts are usually more constrained by task requirements and the social constraints of the situation than novices [though I suggest that experts *recognise* the task requirements and the social constraints rather than that they are constrained by them];

>> experts develop automaticity to allow conscious processing of more complex information; and

>> experts have developed self-regulatory processes as they engage in their activities.

This chapter considers the implications of these in five areas:

1. the development of expertise;

2. how experts structure knowledge;

3. the types of knowledge experts need;

4. how they respond to events and feedback; and

5. how they approach goals in the light of external expectations.

The development of expertise

The list above suggests that expertise is very difficult to develop, requiring a lot of practice over a long period of time. In many fields, such as music and sport, the figure of 10,000 hours is used and Berliner (2004, p 201) cites research that expert radiologists were estimated to have looked at 100,000 X-rays. In relation to teaching, Berliner (2001, p 477) suggests at least four-and-a-half years, though this depends on how expertise is defined and at what level. While this may sound obvious, it contrasts starkly with the view that a teacher can be an expert after a year or two's practice.

Second, expertise develops at an uneven pace, as the individual's understanding changes; and separate aspects of expertise develop at different times and speeds. So a chess player's opening play and his tactical awareness may develop at different rates, probably according to which aspects he practises and concentrates on. And an engineer is likely to acquire expertise more in design, construction, maintenance or repair, according to which she focuses on. While all teachers can, and should be expected to, become increasingly expert, they are unlikely to have a high level of expertise in every respect. Again, obvious, you may think, but too often forgotten.

Third, experts do not just do the same things as novices but better, or quicker, or more economically. They think and operate in different ways. Remember the hockey goalkeeper's expertise. Aspects such as body position, balance and timing were crucial, but this did not just entail doing what a club goalkeeper does, and much better. It involved using and combining varying aspects of knowledge to act in qualitatively different ways. This is less obvious, and understanding the nature of expertise requires considerable experience of the activity involved. So, I can recognise and start to analyse expertise in hockey, teaching and writing far better than in areas such as sailing, law or painting where I have little experience. So, in what follows, it may help to think of an activity at which you are really good and compare your knowledge and actions with those of a beginner.

How experts structure knowledge

One key aspect of expertise is how the individual thinks about problems to be solved. Shulman (2004) provides valuable insights from his work on the thought processes of doctors when diagnosing a patient's medical condition. These processes are usually assumed to be rational, based on collecting all the evidence and then coming to a conclusion on the basis of this. However, Shulman's research suggests that, in practice, doctors intuitively formulate a series of tentative hypotheses, altering these, or formulating new ones, as fresh information becomes available.

A GP to whom I spoke recently stated that she relied heavily on intuition, but added that knowledge of the family often helps to make links which would otherwise be missed, though this could also be a hindrance if one *loses the capacity to be surprised*, in her words, or makes too many presuppositions, in mine. I shall suggest that the primary classteacher's expertise is more like that of the GP than a surgeon, considering and balancing the whole range of the children's, or patients', varying needs.

Such processes are necessary to manage complex situations without oversimplifying, and enabling the expert to concentrate on what really matters, a point to which we return. In Glaser's words (1999, p 91), expertise involves the selective search of memory or use of general problem-solving tactics, with an *efficiency that derives primarily from their knowledge being structured for retrieval, pattern recognition and inferencing.* In other words, their knowledge is arranged so that what matters most can be recalled easily, possible patterns identified and reasonable hypotheses be formulated. Selecting which information or cues to take note of, and which to ignore, is one mark of the real expert.

Shulman (2004) emphasises that, in most fields, experts increasingly work in teams with other people who have specific skills or expertise that they do not have. So, for instance, a surgeon will rely on a whole team, including anaesthetists and specialist nurses; and an architect will work with engineers, quantity surveyors and others. One implication is that different sorts of expertise are – or should be – mutually reinforcing. A second is that responsibility is collective rather than residing with one individual, helping to reduce the sense of isolation and of being on one's own which tends to make one more cautious when faced with uncertainty. However, teachers rarely work in teams – at least when actually teaching – and so are often left isolated in the very situation where they most need the support of others.

The types of knowledge experts need

Let us think what sorts of knowledge an expert needs, by asking who requires the most knowledge – a psychiatrist, a surgeon, a paediatrician, or a general practitioner? Straightaway, one sees that such a question makes little sense. The answer will depend on the type of illness and the person or people being treated. So, diagnosis and treatment of ulcers and heart disease require different types of knowledge, and how one diagnoses and treats an illness may differ for a child and an old person. A general practitioner is likely to have a wider range than a heart surgeon, but in less depth, while the latter has a deeper knowledge, but in a narrower field. Their expertise varies in type or extent rather than amount of knowledge. But this does not stop there being a perceived hierarchy within the profession, with the more specialised knowledge of the surgeon tending to be seen as more prestigious.

We return in Chapter 3 to the different types of knowledge required for teaching, distinguishing between propositional and procedural knowledge – knowing *what* and knowing *how* – and emphasising the role of personal and interpersonal knowledge when dealing with other people. However, for now, remember that, as Berliner (2001, pp 476–77) writes, *case knowledge is a key part of expert knowledge*, continuing that *problems can be classified and solution strategies proposed on the basis of previous experience … [and] when confronted with a new problem, an expert goes through their case knowledge and searches for what Herb Simon has called an 'an old friend', a case like the one now before them.* Expertise depends on gathering, and being able to access, a range of examples which help one to understand and respond to new problems quickly and appropriately, largely based on experience. So, while constantly learning from others, experts are likely to be sceptical, or at least wary, of the latest fad.

Insights from a different profession

Considering how those in another profession work can provide useful insights. A discussion with a family therapist highlighted the following features of how she thought therapists with a high level of expertise operate:

» an ability to maintain momentum and keep to time, so that the session has the necessary 'shape';

» an ability to see and take opportunities which may be less evident to the less-expert practitioner;

» a continuous process of risk assessment;

» a lightness of touch, moving between styles fluidly and gracefully, and without talking too much, while remaining serious about the task;

» a subtle use of language to reframe the client's understanding and to summarise key points;

» an ability to deal with several different factors and tasks simultaneously, recognising what is happening both externally and internally and how these affect each other;

> » an ability to let go of rational, causal thinking at times; and
>
> » authenticity and genuineness, ie this is more than my job.

You may see many similarities and some differences with how a teacher acts, since both therapists and teachers work in a dynamic, constantly changing environment. This requires in-the-moment judgements, often based on intuition, with expertise manifested in relatively small, but important, details.

Berliner (2001, p 478) highlights how in dynamic environments such as nuclear power plants, medical emergency rooms, and air traffic control facilities, expertise is attributed to skills in:

» making accurate inferences about the processes being monitored;

» anticipating outcomes; and

» holding a more global and functional view of the situation.

In these situations, expertise involves avoiding mistakes, since one misjudgement could be disastrous, though separate mechanisms are in place to avoid these. However, teachers can afford to make mistakes. Indeed, I suggest that, like designers, they cannot afford not to take risks, if they are to enhance children's learning or to demonstrate that one learns from one's mistakes at least as much as from one's successes. Those with a high level of expertise do not always 'get it right', though they are quick to know when to adapt.

Expertise is demonstrated in practice, not just in theory. I may be good at all sorts of activities from horse-riding to home economics ... in theory; but hopeless when I actually have to carry them out. So, experts' knowledge is highly procedural, manifested in how they act. Sternberg and Horvath (1995) propose that the best way to understand expertise is as a 'prototype' where there are broad similarities – 'family resemblances' – between experts in the same field but where each individual may demonstrate different behaviours and qualities. In other words, those with a high level of expertise in any one field do not all work in the same way. Expertise is not displayed in actions which can just be copied or 'downloaded' but in types of behaviour which vary according to context and so which require sensitivity to context and judgement.

How experts respond to events and feedback

Bereiter and Scardamalia (cited in Berliner 2001, p 473) distinguish between crystallised and fluid (or adaptive) expertise. The former *consists of intact procedures that have been thoroughly learned through experience, brought forth and used in relatively familiar tasks. Fluid expertise consists of abilities that come into play when an expert confronts novel or challenging tasks.* Those working in complex situations and dynamic environments, such as teachers, require fluid expertise. This involves reliance on intuition and hunch, but supported by a deep knowledge both of the task and the context – and assessment of what might go well or otherwise and noticing signs of whether it is.

Glaser (1999, p 89) writes that *the central underlying properties or meaningful deep structure of the situation is key to experts' perceptions, whereas the surface features and structural properties organise the less-than-expert individuals' perceptions.* This indicates that experts recognise significant patterns and use these to inform practice; and that expertise involves models and routines based on an initial analysis of the situation, but adapted in the light of circumstances. To understand this, it helps me to think about activities at which I am not very good and how I approach them. So, for instance, when putting up a shelf, I usually spend too little time planning, don't have quite the right tools and concentrate on the wrong things. And usually end up calling in an expert to put it right! In contrast, an expert carpenter understands the problem to be solved and works to a plan based on this, while being able and prepared to change when necessary.

Glaser's list on pages 8–9 included *automaticity to allow conscious processing of more complex information.* Experts use routines to help cope with complexity and to decide quickly which information is relevant and which not. For example, the expert doctor or therapist will go through various routine checks and look out for symptoms or responses, especially unexpected ones. Experts know, and try to work at, the limits of their own expertise, but they do so economically, simplifying the situation to make it manageable but without oversimplifying. This allows them to concentrate on, and respond to, what is going on around them. Someone less expert tends to take too much account of what does not matter and either to oversimplify or to adopt an overcomplicated strategy. Oversimplifying limits the opportunities for novelty and improvisation, while overcomplicating leads to confusion and to wasted time.

Experts use self-regulatory processes with great skill, enabling them to step back at appropriate points and observe the process and outcomes of their actions. Their self-awareness is shown in the allocation of attention and sensitivity to what is happening, adapting their initial hypotheses in response to feedback of different types. This is because they need to, and do, see what is not going according to plan, so that they can adapt, with an expert being better than a novice at judging when, and to what extent, an activity or an approach should be modified.

As Sternberg and Horvath (1995, p 16) suggest, an expert *neither jumps into solution attempts prematurely nor follows a solution path blindly … and is able selectively to encode, combine and compare information to arrive at insightful solutions.* So, those with a high level of expertise are likely to move more rapidly to find the best way forward than non-experts when the situation or the problem is relatively simple. However, in complex or unfamiliar territory, they may move more slowly, more deliberatively, testing hypotheses against new evidence, though they are usually likely to be quicker overall and certainly more successful than non-experts. Experts sense when to act and when to hold off, neither panicking nor being indecisive, when faced with uncertainty – and when to stick by the rules and when to bend them.

Let me illustrate this with the example of cooking. A novice is likely to try and follow the recipe exactly. But he may not have the ingredients or the sort of cooker specified, may have to cook several different courses for the same meal and is likely to be anxious. So, however good his planning, he will probably have to adapt quantities or settings and juggle different pans to ensure that everything is cooked at the right time, with his anxiety likely to lead to mistakes. In contrast, the expert cook is able to judge when, whether and how the recipe can be amended and her planning will take account of which dishes can be cooked and left for a while and which must be served straight from the oven. The apparent effortlessness, or at least the ability for anxiety not to induce mistakes, comes in part from an overview of the process gained by previous experience in similar situations.

Another analogy is when trying to find your way in an unfamiliar area. If following travel directions, take one wrong turn and the rest of the directions are useless. When reading a map, it is easy to take what looks like the right path or road and to follow it for a distance even though this does not fit the map. In either case, you have rapidly to be aware when you have started to go wrong. For this, you need to check as the terrain changes, matching the map to the territory. Experts do this regularly and interpret the results accurately. Novices do this too often or not enough and take account of the wrong information. You may argue that a sat-nav or a GPS makes this unnecessary. However, sat-navs can sometimes take you near to your goal but with no way of crossing some intervening barrier and the GPS may break down. So, experts, especially on complex journeys, always have a Plan B to fall back on.

How experts approach goals in the light of external expectations

The expertise of an architect, a doctor and a teacher obviously differ, though there may be some broad similarities, such as attention to the client's needs and well-being or adherence to a code of ethics. So, while expertise is specific to a particular domain, experts' actions are goal-oriented since their thinking and actions are linked to procedures and the rules and conditions for their application. An architect's expertise links goals – say, designing a particular type or style of building – to what is achievable and how it can be achieved. And a sculptor needs not only to design and visualise the final product but to work out which material to use, how to join different parts, where to locate it – and many other small but significant details. Moreover, experts help clients to understand the nature of the task and how it can best be achieved, even though they take account of other, external expectations such as policies and regulations.

While experts may occasionally do brilliant things or have extraordinary insights, for the most part, they do ordinary things extremely well, so that what they do ceases to be ordinary. So, an expert recognises what is to be achieved, whether it can be and the best way(s) of doing so. This may be (relatively) simple when there is only one main goal – to hit the bullseye and to make a beautiful pot – though this is difficult consistently and under pressure. However, the more complex the situation, the more there are likely to be competing imperatives. For example, while a potter may wish to make and glaze a bowl in particular ways, time constraints – and the need to earn a living – may mean that he is not able to spend as long on this as he might wish.

The nature of expertise depends heavily on the level of predictability. Chess pieces and machines move according to predictable rules. People – especially young children – do not. When working with people, there will often be situations where long-term objectives clash with short-term ones. So, the mother of a young child may know that ideally she should patiently explain why he should or should not act in a certain way, but having to get to nursery or look after another child may make this impossible – so that no course of action will meet both short- and long-term objectives exactly.

An expert in a complex social situation, like a courtroom or a classroom, recognises that there are many different goals, and types of goal, and will balance short-term objectives and long-term goals, over time; but with a view to the bigger picture. As a result, expertise in such situations involves making choices about priorities, complying with what is required externally, when necessary, but always seeking to prioritise the client's needs.

We tend to assume that expertise can be seen by watching someone for a short period. In some cases, this is true. A musician's or a surgeon's expertise is demonstrated on every occasion that they perform. However, expertise also resides in longer sequences, especially when working with people. So, a barrister is not judged on making one brilliant speech or an engineer on designing one piece of a complex structure. Success is determined by whether the case is won or the structure operates safely. In teaching a class, I suggest, expertise must be understood not just on the quality of one lesson or the outcomes of a test, but over a long period of time and on how a group of children with a wide range of interests, aptitudes and personalities learn.

IN A **NUTSHELL**

Ruthven et al.'s (2004, p 2) analysis of the key aspects of expertise in complex social situations indicates that the research literature shows that experts have acquired intuitive specialist knowledge to meet the demands of everyday situations (Ericsson and Smith, 1991). Such 'knowledge in action' is interwoven with the social, physical and cultural context in which activity and learning take place (Brown et al., 1989). Thus, expertise is tuned to the setting and shaped by structuring resources available in the situation (Lave, 1988). Equally, expertise incorporates an important degree of flexibility and the capacity to respond to the uncertainty and contingency which are normal in real-life situations (Wynne, 1991).

This indicates that expertise is 'situated' and so specific to the context in which it is exercised, and should be seen as prototypical – that is within broad, fluid boundaries to take account of individual difference and not manifested in the same way by everyone or by the same person in every situation. Since expertise is largely tacit and intuitive, its features are often not easily articulated either by the expert or by an observer – and so become evident only with detailed observation, over time. Therefore, describing it requires careful, in-depth analysis with reference to the particular context. While there are some generic features of expertise in any domain, many are context dependent. For teachers, this is not only teaching in general but the age group, subject and setting. So, in the next chapter, we turn more specifically to teacher expertise, before considering young children and the primary classroom.

REFLECTIONS ON **CRITICAL ISSUES**

- *Experts appear to work without great effort, but this is hard for those less expert to replicate.*
- *Since expertise is prototypical, experts may work in different ways when approaching a similar task.*
- *Since expertise is situated, it is specific to a particular area of activity, though some general lessons can be learned from comparable areas.*
- *Since expertise is largely tacit, it is very hard to identify its features in ourselves or other people, though fairly easy to recognise.*
- *Teachers tend to think their own challenges are unique, as they are, but there is much to learn from those in other professions dealing with complex social situations.*
- *Expertise develops over time, and unevenly.*

CRITICAL **ISSUES**

- To what extent is 'outstanding' teaching defined differently according to culture?
- Which types of knowledge are most important in teaching?
- How do teachers with a high level of expertise act?
- Why is the teacher's judgement so important in teaching?
- What is the basis for how teachers with a high level of expertise act?

Introduction

Expertise in teaching is very hard to describe, because of the complexity of the classroom and the relationships and interactions within it; and because an observer is unlikely to know what has happened before and certainly not what follows. Yet, as Sternberg and Horvath suggest (1995, p 8), *to know what we are developing teachers toward, we need a model of teaching expertise.* Since expertise is prototypical, teachers with a high level of expertise act in different ways, but this chapter explores areas of similarity. It draws on research to identify key features of expertise in teaching, looking at different types of knowledge, interactions with children and attitudes and beliefs, in resolving the dilemmas inherent in teaching. First, three difficulties in identifying the features of teacher expertise must be recognised.

Three difficulties

Can expertise be assessed in one lesson?

One assumption underlying Ofsted's approach to inspection is that one can assess accurately how good a teacher is on the basis on observing one lesson, or even part of a lesson. Inspectors with a high level of expertise can make hypotheses informed by their experience, but they see only a snapshot. As Shulman (2004, p 396) writes, *most of the embarrassments of pedagogy that I encounter are not the inability of teachers to teach well, for an hour or even a day. Rather they flow from an inability to sustain episodes of teaching and learning over time that unfold, accumulate, into meaningful understanding in students.*

Cooper and McIntyre (1996, pp 78–82) highlight that the skilled teachers whom they studied balanced long-term aims, over an extended time scale, with short-term objectives. While such teachers may focus their own, and their children's efforts, on a particular skill or activity, they see, and work towards, the big picture, not just aiming for short-term success, but laying the foundations for the future. Just as one would not judge a garden designer on only the quality of the rockery or the vegetable patch, teacher expertise should be assessed not just on one lesson or one topic but more holistically. It involves maintaining a consistently high standard over time, not just meeting short-term objectives or putting on a good demonstration lesson.

Does teaching expertise vary between cultures?

Troman (1996, p 33) writes: *[d]efinitions of teacher quality and the 'good' teacher are social constructions and subject to change at different historical moments.* And Berliner (2001, p 467): *the cognitive competencies of expert teachers must always be thought of as relative to a culture, since what constitutes expert teaching will change in some cultures quite rapidly.* Alexander (2000) documented in detail considerable differences between what counted as good teaching in five different systems. So, teachers of young children in Russia engaged in whole-class discussions, those in India relied mainly on a didactic approach and those in the United States allowed more independent exploration.

While context affects expertise in teaching much more than in activities like ice skating or bridge, I shall challenge the view that teacher expertise is quite so dependent on culture. Cultures and systems may encourage particular teaching styles; and individual teachers, inevitably, have preferred styles. But teaching styles must be adapted according to what the teacher wishes to achieve. For example, teaching the periodic table and how to conduct a scientific experiment are likely to require different approaches; and teaching subtraction may require presenting this in a range of ways to help different children understand when to subtract as well as how to do so. Teachers with a high level of expertise strive to achieve many goals, and by different routes, rather than just those deemed to matter, or prescribed, by other people.

I suggest that teacher expertise operates at three levels, of which the teaching style is only one. Teaching style may depend heavily on what is expected or on personal preference – and should vary depending on what is to be learned. So this must be related to aims, for instance to encourage an individual child to apply his or her skills, or provide a group with an appropriate range of experiences to extend their horizons or learn to work together. Whatever the teaching style, expertise depends on the interactions between teacher and learners, in ways to be discussed shortly. But these levels are interlinked, so that teaching style will reflect, and be affected by, what the teacher hopes to achieve; and the detail of how a teacher interacts with the class cannot be separated from the objectives of the lesson and from the style of pedagogy adopted.

Can one separate one's beliefs about expertise from those about education?

Perhaps the hardest aspect of recognising teacher expertise, as a teacher or an observer, is separating this from one's own beliefs about pedagogy or about education. We all feel an affinity with a particular style or approach and have our own prejudices, both individually and as a culture. However, since teacher expertise is prototypical, there is no one 'right' way. Many teachers with a high level of expertise work in ways that I could not, or would not wish to. Ultimately, though, teaching must be judged on how well it enhances learning for particular individuals and classes.

There is a danger in any attempt to generalise about teaching. However, there is an even greater danger in not trying to do so – saying that what makes a good teacher cannot be identified or, even worse, that some teachers 'just are' good and do not have to work at improving their teaching. So, the rest of this chapter looks in more detail at what I call the fabric of pedagogy, the details that combine to create the whole tapestry, to try and identify what is distinctive about teachers with a high level of expertise.

Key areas of teacher expertise

Glaser (1999, pp 96–100) highlights four key themes associated with teacher expertise:

1. the nature of practice;
2. self-monitoring skills;
3. principled performance; and
4. the social context of learning.

These are all themes to which we return.

Bond et al's research (see Berliner, 2001, p 469) identifies 13 prototypical areas, which I have re-ordered and grouped under five headings.

Bond's prototypical areas

Teacher knowledge

» *better use of knowledge;*

» *extensive pedagogical content knowledge, including deep representations of subject matter.*

Setting objectives and providing feedback

» *more challenging objectives;*

» *better monitoring of learning and providing feedback to students;*

» *better adaptation and modifications of goals for diverse learners, including better skills for improvisation.*

Understanding and responding to events

» *better perception of classroom events, including a better ability to read cues from students;*

» *better problem-solving strategies;*

» *more frequent testing of hypotheses;*

» *better decision-making.*

Climate and context

» *better classroom climate;*

» *greater sensitivity to context.*

Attitude and beliefs

» *greater respect for students;*

» *display of more passion for teaching.*

Commenting on these, Alexander (2010, p 418) states that they were *correlated with measures such as students' higher levels of achievement, deep rather than surface understanding of subject matter, higher motivation to learn and feelings of self-efficacy,* especially with younger and low-income pupils, a point discussed further in Chapter 5.

While such categories form a basis for exploring how teachers with a high level of expertise act and think, 'better' does not help much, since it is by definition better to be better. Terms such as 'more frequent' or 'more extensive' help identify how such teachers operate and the attributes and qualities they demonstrate. So, as we explore these areas in more detail, let us try to be more precise.

Teacher knowledge

You can probably recall a teacher who was tremendously knowledgeable about his or her subject, but not a good teacher. A brilliant musician or writer may not be a good teacher of music or writing. Indeed, it may be – and I believe often is – that those who understand the difficulties learners encounter are those best positioned to help them overcome these. Teachers with a high level of expertise can demonstrate, explain, analyse and correct errors, and much else besides, based on understanding of different learners' strategies. The expert non-teacher or the less-expert teacher has a smaller repertoire. Take, for example, someone with too much knowledge of how a computer works to recognise the gaps in a beginner's knowledge; or how an expert sportsplayer may not recognise basic mistakes or bad habits – of body position, or footwork, or grip – which hamper a beginner's progress or later development, if not corrected at an early stage. In teaching young children, the equivalent is to notice how a five year-old is holding the pencil, when a seven year-old does not realise that a fraction is part of a whole or when a nine year-old changes more than one variable in a science experiment.

We tend to equate knowledge with information – propositional knowledge. However, this is not much use (except in pub quizzes and exams) unless one can apply this. A second type – procedural knowledge – involves being able to do' something in practice rather than just in theory. This was captured by the Ancient Greeks in their term *phronesis* – usually translated as practical wisdom. I 'know', in theory, how to do many practical activities, from mending a puncture to growing vegetables, and from devising a good lesson plan to engaging disruptive children; but achieving these in practice is hard. This requires not just propositional and procedural, but personal and interpersonal, knowledge. As Elliott et al. (2011, p 85) indicate, skilled interpersonal relations are crucial for effective teaching and learning. Knowledge of others and of oneself, one's strengths and shortcomings, is one mark of teachers with a high level of expertise, especially when working with less experienced learners.

Much of the research on teacher expertise emphasises a deep understanding of the subject, such as history or maths. This is likely to matter more with older children as they grapple with complex ideas, but even more important is the notion of match – finding the best ways to present material to a child or group of children at a particular stage of development or understanding. Shulman describes this as pedagogical content knowledge – often shortened subsequently to PCK – defining this (2004, p 203) as a *particular form of content knowledge that embodies the aspect of content most germane to its teachability … the most useful forms of representation … the most powerful analogies, illustrations, examples, explanations and demonstrations – in a word, the ways of formulating the subject that make it comprehensible to others.* While Shulman, and others such as Turner-Bissett (1999, 2001), break PCK into several different elements, I find this simple definition very useful.

Recalling the analogy with surgeons and GPs, I suggest that primary classteachers may not need – or be able – to have a really deep understanding of maths and history, of art and literature, of science and physical education. They need *enough* understanding of these (for a particular age group or class), but this has to be complemented by PCK and other elements of professional knowledge. Such knowledge is often categorised as domain and craft knowledge. The former is often implicitly equated with subject knowledge, such as geography, science or religious education, reinforcing the questionable idea that the best teachers are those with the greatest subject knowledge, regardless of who is being taught and in what context. Since teaching is a practical activity, it can be characterised as a craft, but this may lead one to underplay the extent to which teaching has the intellectual rigour of a science and the fluidity of an art. Grimmett and Mackinnon (1992, p 437) argue that *craft knowledge is vastly different from the packaged and glossy maxims that govern 'the science of education' … Craft knowledge has a different sort of rigour, one that places more confidence in the judgement of teachers, their feel for the work, their love for students and learning.* To explore craft knowledge, we turn to how teachers with a high level of expertise approach teaching – what they really do in the classroom.

Setting objectives and providing feedback

Anyone can set challenging objectives. The difficulty, though, is to set the right kind, appropriate to individual children, and to a whole group or class, both for the short and the long term. This involves matching activities closely to individual children's – and a whole group's – current levels of capability, not only cognitively, but in areas like problem solving, teamwork and creativity – and adapting these if need be. So, monitoring and assessing learning are essential elements of teaching, not separate activities.

Monitoring learning, that is checking constantly how and what children are learning, rather than what they are doing or how they are behaving, is difficult. This is not just because of the busy-ness of the classroom but because it requires a range of strategies – questioning, listening, watching, interpreting and many more – which pay attention to learning processes. Doing so also requires the assurance to change course, rather than ploughing on regardless. For instance, Schemp et al. (1998, p 351) suggest that *expert physical education teachers have a kind of 'plan independence', when teaching in areas of their pedagogical strength ... and had the ability to accommodate a range of learner skills and abilities, appeared more flexible and opportunistic, and demonstrated a willingness to change activities whenever they deemed it appropriate.* Teachers with a high level of expertise modify goals and adapt activities constantly for particular children – or groups – in the light of their prior learning and their responses and enable children increasingly to do so for themselves.

Teachers with a high level of expertise are able to observe and adapt their own actions. To do this, they must be attuned to children's feelings and behaviours and attend to what the children do and say, rather than focusing mainly on themselves. Berliner (2001, p 476) cites Ropo's finding that *novices concentrate[d] on their own behaviour and management of the lesson, while experts seemed to pay more attention to the content of students' answers.* This enables teaching to be reciprocal and interactive, rather than one-way and transmissive.

Teachers with a high level of expertise do not equate assessment with testing. They take account of test scores, but their assessments are tentative and based on a much wider bank of evidence, in particular that of progress rather than of absolute scores and knowledge of the child and the context. Seeing assessment as primarily to enhance children's learning and integral to the process of teaching enables teachers to provide formative feedback. This involves confirming what has been done well, correcting errors and identifying 'next steps', looking back in order to see the way ahead. A tick or a grade does little to achieve this, whereas a comment or a suggestion may clarify a misunderstanding or help to open up new avenues. Moreover, much feedback is informal, often unconscious. Teachers are not giving feedback only when consciously doing so. A gesture of approval, a frown, a sigh, a pause, are all elements of how they help to shape, support or suppress children's learning.

Understanding and responding to events

We have seen how experts adopt the strategy most likely to resolve a particular problem and constantly test hypotheses to see how well this is working. This applies to teachers, but makes the process seem rather static. Chapter 2 introduced the idea of fluid expertise, to respond rapidly but appropriately to a dynamic, constantly changing environment. Schon (1987) distinguishes between reflection-on-action and reflection-in-action. Reflection-on-action is useful in planning and evaluating, but what distinguishes teachers with a high level of expertise is the ability to reflect-in-action, think on their feet, to make appropriate decisions rapidly. This matters particularly when expecting children to be active in their learning.

While most teachers reflect on what they have done, reflection-in-action involves flexibility and improvisation, but not an unplanned or random approach. Sawyer (2004, p 13) describes this as 'disciplined improvisation', in contrast to 'scripted instruction', with teachers able to improvise within broad structures and frameworks in ways that they could justify, if required. Such teachers may not always act in ways that seem predictable or consistent, but they could if need be – and often may – explain why not. For instance, they may respond to one interruption but not to another, similar one, depending on the individual and the context. Or spend more time with one group at the expense of another, often based on intuition.

Eraut (2000, p 258) argues that expertise, especially in teaching, consists of the ability to act rapidly and appropriately, with intuitive processes usually coming first, but backed up, when need be, by analytic and deliberative ones. As Bruner (1960, p 58) indicates, *intuitive thinking characteristically does not advance in careful, well-planned steps. Indeed, it tends to involve manoeuvres based seemingly on an implicit perception of the total problem. The thinker arrives at an answer, which may be right or wrong, with little if any awareness of the process by which he reached it.* Teachers may step back to think more analytically, but they mostly work fluidly on hunch, rather like the doctors in Chapter 2. How teachers with a high level of expertise act, and why, at that moment, in that way, may not be obvious either to the individual or to someone watching. It has become so internalised that it is 'second nature', rather like 'muscle memory'. In Pollard's words (2010, p 5), *the more expert a teacher becomes, the more his/her expertise is manifested in sensitivity to contexts and situations, in imaginative judgements in-the-moment sourced from tacit knowledge.*

John (2000, pp 98–101) identifies five important aspects of how student teachers demonstrate their level of expertise:

> » problem avoidance;
>
> » interpretation of pupil cues;
>
> » opportunity creation;
>
> » improvisation; and
>
> » mood assessment.

These are examples of what I call the fabric of pedagogy, whatever the approach adopted. These imply different, more interactive and fluid qualities than a model based on detailed planning and delivery, with clear learning objectives made explicit to the class.

Avoiding a problem – a case study

Let me give an example of problem avoidance and interpreting cues. As a headteacher, I went to mention something to the teacher. As she was talking to one child, I saw a nine year-old behind her, just about to throw something across the room. While I hesitated, she called out, without turning her head, 'Oh! Martin, could you come and help me?' The child I had been watching came straight over and was delighted to undertake a small task; and then settle back down to his work. I have often thought of this remarkable yet ordinary incident, managing to avoid a problem and consequent disruption, by a simple, timely and non-confrontational intervention. I wonder whether you can think of similar examples of how a teacher noticed a cue and so avoided a difficult situation.

Problem avoidance may involve grouping children or arranging resources in ways which present fewer opportunities for conflict or wasted time; or intervening just before a silly remark. Anticipating possible outcomes is one indicator of teacher expertise. Interpretation of pupil cues may range from recognising when an individual does not grasp a concept to when a group has started a task in an unexpected way – and deciding whether to encourage or discourage this – to judging if the class is benefiting from an impromptu discussion and the next planned activity should be abandoned. This often requires improvising in ways which are 'semi-planned', but can be justified on the basis of previous experience and an overview of learning which avoids a dogmatic sticking-to-the-plan. This involves some risk but without such risk children's learning is likely to be inhibited.

Of the five aspects above, assessment of mood is perhaps the hardest but most vital in teaching a class of young children. It is the most intuitive and can lead rapidly to a loss of control, when misjudged, or to memorable learning experiences, when done well. So, for instance, expecting a group of six year-olds to measure the perimeter of the field or allowing them to build a model of a Roman fort may lead to wasted time or to new insights, depending on the calmness or otherwise of the class and whether members of a group can work well together – and likewise with composing a piece of music or researching the history of slavery with a class of 11 year-olds. Teachers with a high level of expertise have a 'lightness of touch' – an apparent ability to move easily between different approaches and levels, like the therapist in Chapter 2, and a sense of timing, when to intervene, when to hold back, like an actor, depending on the emotional climate of the class. These attributes are partly why teacher expertise is so hard for others to see – and even harder to learn and sustain.

Creating a climate and context for learning

Meeting the needs, both academic and otherwise, of a class of around 30 children with a wide diversity of personalities, abilities and experiences is a challenge for all classteachers. They have a key role in identifying children's strengths to be built on and obstacles to be overcome if all children, whatever their background, are to be included and have the chance to succeed. Some classes include children with an obvious mix of ethnicity, language, religion and socio-economic backgrounds – and increasingly those with physical disabilities or with behavioural or other needs. Others may appear more homogeneous. However, all classes contain children with a range of different needs, and – more than many teachers recognise – difficult backgrounds, such as abuse or domestic violence, racism or poverty, or significant responsibilities, such as caring for other family members. Therefore, creating an inclusive classroom is an essential part of any classteacher's role.

As Shulman (2004, pp 378–79) writes, *teachers not only represent the content of their disciplines; they model the processes of inquiry and analysis, the attitudes and dispositions of scholarship and criticism, and they purposively create communities of interaction and discourse within which ideas are created, exchanged and evaluated.* This may sound rather grand for young children but it indicates that:

>> example and role models;

>> children learning to work in particular ways and develop particular qualities; and

>> communities of learners;

are all vital aspects of what teachers can influence – the climate and context for learning most appropriate for that particular group. This involves for all teachers:

>> engaging and including children with different backgrounds, abilities and aptitudes;

>> providing an appropriate balance of activities; and

>> selecting the most appropriate teaching approaches.

But other aspects will vary, depending on what is being taught, the children's age and the nature and size of the group. Since what makes for a good climate and context for learning is so dependent on these, a detailed discussion of what this entails for the primary classteacher is left until Chapters 4 and 5.

Dilemmas and patterns of resolution

Berlak and Berlak (1981, pp 22–3) outline a series of dilemmas, which they see as inherent in how any teacher acts. Some are related to who – the child or the teacher – controls time, activities and standards. Some are to do with questions such as whether knowledge is presented as given or problematic, and learning as individual or social and as holistic or in small bits. Some relate to whether teachers see children as intrinsically or extrinsically motivated and whether children should all be treated the same or allowances made for some, for instance, in allocating resources and in applying rules. These are dilemmas because no one answer is applicable to every situation. Perhaps you can think of other examples.

Berlak and Berlak argue that teachers have to find 'patterns of resolution' for these dilemmas. This entails finding the right balance between the ends of a continuum for each dilemma. For instance, this might involve deciding how much time to allocate to particular groups of children, and which ones; or how much to set definite objectives or to allow children to exercise their own creativity. But teachers also have to balance different dilemmas. So, in responding to a child who has misbehaved, the teacher makes judgements based not only on policies and procedures, but on an understanding of the child's background, the impact on other children and the particular situation. Where it may be appropriate to reprimand one child publicly, a quiet word may be best for another in a similar situation; and how the teacher responds to the same individual in different situations may, rightly, vary. As Alexander writes (1995, p 67) *teaching is essentially a series of compromises.*

Teaching children, especially young ones, is inherently unpredictable, unless the teacher controls the situation so closely that there is little scope for creativity, or for exploring child-generated questions and ideas. Teachers with a high level of expertise make the situation manageable for themselves by establishing routines and expectations so that they can concentrate on what matters most. In McEwan's words (1997, p 141), *the predictable becomes, by definition, background, leaving the attention uncluttered, the better to deal with the random or unexpected.* However, in doing so, such teachers do not oversimplify what children are expected to do. For example, they establish clear boundaries on behaviour and classroom routines, but expect children to speculate, to question, to challenge. They create rather than just deliver a curriculum, complying with external expectations but only to some extent. This is because principled performance, recalling Glaser's term (1999, pp 98–9), involves prioritising children's learning needs, not those of teachers or the system.

Teachers with a high level of expertise take account of how opportunities and challenges vary, depending on factors such as the children's age and background. So, teaching six year-olds and ten year-olds, or in a large inner-city or a small rural primary school, require different types of expertise. The intellectual challenges are likely to be greater with 11 year-olds than with five year-olds and the emotional ones greater with the younger age group. And the pressures resulting from how children behave may be more intense in a disadvantaged area, those from parental expectations in a more affluent one. This may entail adopting different pedagogies for particular groups, for instance giving additional opportunities and encouragement to enable boys to work successfully in groups or girls to be more assertive; and opportunities for those from disadvantaged backgrounds to have additional access to experiences which otherwise they might miss. Such issues may be controversial, but these are dilemmas to be considered in creating an inclusive learning environment.

Teacher attitudes and beliefs

So far, this chapter has concentrated on what teachers do. Sometimes, what they refrain from doing matters as much as what they do, such as not interrupting, interfering or inhibiting. Expertise is manifested less in *what* teachers do, than in *how* they act, doing ordinary things well, rather than acting in unusual ways. So, teachers with a high level of expertise:

- » observe *carefully*;
- » listen *attentively*;
- » talk *sparingly*;
- » explain *clearly*;
- » question *insightfully*;
- » wait *patiently*;
- » respond *thoughtfully*; and
- » challenge *gently*.

You should be able to add to the list, but pay particular attention to the adverbs.

Drawing on funds of knowledge

Teachers' attitudes and beliefs influence not just what they do or don't do, but how they do it. For instance, Bond et al. (see Berliner, 2001, p 469) highlighted 'greater respect for students'. Too often, teachers show little respect for children and what they know, especially where this does not fit with what schools deem to be valuable. Even at a young age, children often have considerable knowledge about, and experience of, activities which are not part of the formal curriculum – such as languages spoken at home, computer games and fishing – of which teachers, and the school system, take little notice. Some children have fewer resources than others to draw on in school, not only in terms of language or computers, or breadth of opportunity and availability of parental support, but in how their culture and knowledge, their experiences and interests are regarded. In academic language, their 'cultural capital' – a term discussed further in Eaude (2011, pp 85–88) – and their funds of knowledge, based on their life experiences, are different from that which schools value. Teachers with a high level of expertise respect and draw on these funds of knowledge. They do not patronise children by treating them as blank slates, but see them as powerful, if inexperienced, learners, recognising and building on existing strengths.

One vital aspect of teaching is to believe in children, not to give up on them, to keep hope alive. This entails maintaining high expectations of all children, which helps raise their aspirations. This is harder than it appears. Teachers, often unconsciously, adapt their expectations on the basis of ethnicity, gender and background, and of perceived ability. Certainly, I, to my shame, have done so, though I have consciously struggled against this. As Ireson et al. (1999, p 216) write,

high expectations ... have to spring naturally from the belief and aspirations of the teacher and learner. They have to be genuine or they become counterproductive ... Expectations are passed between teacher and learner in subtle, often undetected, ways ... Underpinning teachers' attitudes to the capabilities of their students is their belief about intelligence ... If ... teachers believe that intelligence can be modified by experience, they will be more likely to pitch their expectations positively.

Encouraging a growth mind-set

Dweck (2000, pp 5–6) contrasts two distinct reactions to failure – what she calls the helpless and mastery-oriented patterns. In brief, helpless is the view that once failure occurs, the situation is out of one's control and nothing can be done. Mastery-oriented refers to the *hardy response to failure because ... students remained focused on achieving mastery in spite of their present difficulties.* This is linked to whether a learner has a 'fixed' or a 'growth' mind-set, whether he sees intelligence as fixed or able to be enhanced by greater experience and effort. And this is profoundly influenced by the teacher's attitudes and responses, since how children learn depends heavily on relationships and what is encouraged (or otherwise) by teachers.

Dweck argues that children should be praised for behaviours, such as trying hard, being persistent or co-operating, rather than for intelligence. This helps the child (and the class) to see that success is not just about performance and outcomes nor is it only the result of being innately clever or not. I find it hard to see how any teacher who does not believe that experience can help develop untapped, maybe unknown, areas of ability could be regarded as having a high level of expertise. In other words, education is transformative rather than simply performative. Hart et al. (2004) and Swann et al. (2012) provide excellent and readable accounts of the implications for practice.

Creating a curriculum

Ofsted (2010, p 4), in evaluating and illustrating how 44 schools in all phases used creative approaches to learning, suggest that in almost all *most of the teachers felt confident in encouraging pupils to make connections across traditional boundaries, speculate constructively, maintain an open mind while exploring a wider range of options, and reflect critically on ideas and outcomes.* Teaching is a creative activity and confidence a key feature of teacher expertise. So, teachers with a high level of expertise recognise that a curriculum is not just a syllabus to be delivered but a programme to be developed – a guide rather than a straitjacket. So, they see themselves as curriculum developers, not deliverers. They tweak the formal curriculum. They trust their judgement to ensure children's engagement by providing a broad range of activities and experiences and using different ways of presenting material and ideas. For primary classteachers, this involves weaving together the vertical threads, progression in different subject areas, and the horizontal, cross-disciplinary ones, the warp and weft of the curriculum tapestry, over time. So, they are constantly aware of – and on the look-out for – connections and helping children to do so.

Chapter 4 explores the primary classteacher's role, to gain insight into what makes the task so complicated and why it is so hard to teach with confidence, providing the basis for discussion in Chapter 5 of what the classteacher's expertise entails when working with young children.

IN A **NUTSHELL**

Outstanding teaching tends currently to be understood as involving lessons meticulously planned to meet specific, predetermined objectives. In contrast, this chapter has presented teaching as:

» inherently complex with expertise involving being able to respond appropriately to the uncertainties inevitably involved;

» reciprocal and often intuitive and improvised; and

» requiring an attention to small details, with these and styles of teaching linked to overall aims and immediate objectives.

While some aspects of teacher expertise are generic, such as being able to inspire children, use time efficiently, control a class or encourage learners to do their best, these are too general to be of much use in deciding what these imply in practice. The view presented from the research sees expertise as a combination of the detail of classroom interactions and of teaching strategies to meet a broad set of long-term goals which may vary for different children. Teachers with a high level of expertise create and sustain a climate and environment for learning and within that choose from a repertoire of strategies depending on what they hope to achieve. So, they are constantly making judgements to find patterns of resolution to a series of often-conflicting dilemmas.

REFLECTIONS ON **CRITICAL ISSUES**

* *Each culture tends to privilege particular approaches to teaching, but much of teacher expertise consists of being able to see the big picture while attending carefully to details.*
* *Expertise in teaching requires many different types of knowledge, including subject, procedural and personal/interpersonal knowledge.*
* *Teachers with a high level of expertise are particularly skilled not only at deciding what to do in advance, but in adapting and responding to events.*
* *Expertise in teaching involves recognising and resolving a range of dilemmas, creating and sustaining an environment and climate for teaching and learning.*
* *Teachers with a high level of expertise believe in, and find ways to enable, all children's abilities to learn, even when it is hard to do so.*

CRITICAL **ISSUES**

- *In which respects are the primary classteacher's aims distinctive from those of other teachers?*
- *Which aspects of how young children learn most affect how primary classteachers work?*
- *What, in the classroom, makes teaching a class of young children so challenging?*
- *How do external expectations influence how primary classteachers work?*
- *How do all of these combine to affect how primary classteachers teach and think about themselves?*

Introduction

The primary classteacher's role may seem obvious: to teach a group of children, usually of the same age, often supported by one or more other adults, for all or most of the school week and to ensure that they gain a sound grasp of literacy and numeracy. This chapter suggests that the role is more complicated and the aims broader than this, including motivating and empowering a wide range of children, taking account of the different ways in which young children learn, and that the constraints on doing so are considerable.

The first two sections discuss the aims of the primary classteacher and key points about how young children learn. This is followed by a consideration of the social and emotional factors operating in a class of young children, and then of external expectations, and the effect of these factors on how primary classteachers think and work. The final section considers the wider role of the primary classteacher, beyond the classroom.

Aims

The aims of education are multiple and complex, including aspects such as social and emotional well-being and character, values and identity; and enabling children not only to understand and appreciate the world as it is but how it may be in the future. This is enshrined in legislation such as the 2011 Education Act and the new Ofsted Framework, which re-assert the importance of spiritual, moral, social and cultural development (SMSC), the implications of which are discussed in Eaude (2008). This may involve challenging, and helping children to question, widely held assumptions within society, for instance, about attitudes towards people who are different or what constitutes success or well-being, and how to achieve this. So, classteachers with a high level of expertise do not see their role only in terms of academic attainment.

A teacher of A level chemistry or English may concentrate mainly on building up subject and procedural knowledge – ways of thinking and working as a scientist or a critical reader – and ensuring good results in exams. Those working with young children have to help children develop subject and procedural knowledge in many different subject areas, rather than only in mathematics or design and technology, for example – albeit not in such great depth. Moreover, given the age of the children, they must pay particular attention to aspects associated with SMSC, including emotional regulation, social development and the exploration of culture and identity – questions such as Who am I? How should I act and interact? Where do I belong? – building on, and building up, broad and deep foundations for life-long and life-wide learning.

Bone (2010) suggests that young children should:

- » *be* accepted for what they are rather than just for what they may become;
- » *become* transformed through the activities and experiences they encounter; and
- » *belong* to larger entities and groups.

Classteachers have a pivotal role in helping young children to belong in a world more complex and confusing than that in which their teachers grew up, where many children are uncertain about where and how they fit in. Many children, if they miss out on experiences which extend them, socially, culturally and aesthetically as well as intellectually, will never have such opportunities again. In a culture where there are strong pressures for children to grow up too quickly, teachers must offer children chances just to 'be' children, by which I mean exploring, experiencing and enjoying childhood, rather than always being driven to 'become' – preparing, often anxiously, for an uncertain future. Achieving this requires a deep knowledge of young children, how they learn and the context in which they grow up.

Five key points about how young children learn

The TLRP (see page 4) suggested that learning processes do not fundamentally change with age, though contexts do, and that more attention should be paid to learning relationships. This section highlights five often-overlooked aspects of how young children learn:

1. the link between cognitive and emotional processes;
2. how relationships support active meaning-making;

3. children's needs for different means of representation;

4. being cared-for and caring-for; and

5. the power of example.

The link between cognitive and emotional processes

As Gerhardt (2004, p 24) writes, *unconsciously acquired, non-verbal patterns and expectations ... are inscribed in the brain outside conscious awareness, in the period of infancy and ... underpin our behaviour in relationships through life*. For instance, theory about infant attachment (see Eaude, 2011, p 48) emphasises the significance of anxiety in determining responses and the importance of predictable relationships in helping to contain anxiety at a manageable level. Without this, children (and indeed all of us) tend either to withdraw or to become aggressive. Children enjoy challenge but must feel safe to explore, to take risks, to create.

A great deal of research, such as that summarised in Rogoff (1990) and Cooper and McIntyre (1996, pp 90–91), indicates how the cognitive and emotional aspects of learning are closely interlinked, like the strands of a rope. So, children who feel safe are better placed to learn, but anxiety can easily block conscious processes. Unless learners are protected from the emotional cost of failure, especially the public cost, they are unlikely to take risks and conscious mechanisms become ineffective. When I tried to learn to sing, at the age of 40, I knew what to do, but anxiety meant that I was unable to sing. For an eight year-old, this may mean that he knows how to behave, but is unable to make the conscious choices which his teacher expects. So, classteachers must be aware of how learning is affected by unconscious processes, often the result of previous experience and the immediate environment.

How relationships support active meaning-making

Bruner (1996) and Rogoff (1990) emphasise that from early infancy children are active meaning-makers, supported by those who care for them. Their development depends on reciprocal relationships. Just think how a young child learns to speak – by a complex process of listening, rehearsing, trying, being corrected, self-correcting, with parents/carers talking, and responding to, his emerging patterns of speech. As Donaldson (1982, 1992) showed, young children's responses depend very strongly on the context of a task and the trust they have with the person setting it. And as Rogoff (1990, pp 94–95) suggests, *[i]nvolvement in the overall process and purpose of the activity, in a manageable and supported form, gives children a chance to see how the steps fit together and to participate in aspects of the activity that reflect the overall goals, gaining both skills and a vision of how and why the activity works.*

In Salzberger-Wittenberg et al.'s words (1983, p ix), *our learning, in infancy and for a considerable period, takes place within a dependent relationship to another human being. It is the quality of the relationship which deeply influences the hopefulness required to remain curious and open to new experiences, the capacity to perceive connections and to discover their meaning.* Older children may become less dependent on relationships, but these remain highly influential throughout the primary years, and beyond. The more unsure or insecure the learner, the more continuity of relationships matters, whereas more confident learners can cope with change more easily. Learning depends on social interaction, especially what Rogoff (1990) describes as 'guided participation' where a less experienced learner works alongside a more experienced one. How this happens and how children understand and engage with the activity affects their motivation and their learning. Such support is often described as scaffolding, but this must be both intellectual and emotional, maintain cognitive challenge rather than oversimplify the task and be temporary if it is not to create dependence.

Different means of representing experience

One respect in which young children's minds differ from those of adults is their ability to think abstractly. As Black (1999, p 121) writes, *one of Piaget's principles that still commands acceptance is that we learn by actions, by self-directed problem-solving aimed at trying to control the world and that abstract thought evolves from concrete action.* In Piaget's words (cited in Papert, 1999), *children have real understanding only of that which they invent themselves and each time that we try to teach them something too quickly we keep them from re-inventing it themselves.* So, they are active agents, constantly building on their previous patterns of understanding.

Bruner (2006, volume 1, p 69) suggests that learning depends on how past experience is coded and processed, which he calls representations of experience, of which he identifies three main types:

> » the enactive, through actions;
>
> » the iconic, through visual means; and
>
> » the symbolic, through symbols, especially language.

Vygotsky (1978) argued that conceptual development occurs primarily through interaction, especially with those with greater experience, through the use of tools, notably language. This interaction enhances how children think and learn the metacognition – thinking about thinking – which helps them to relate the specific to the general. Adults tend to assume that thinking should be individual and precede action. But thinking is often best done with others, especially at the limits of one's current understanding, to help both to clarify one's own thoughts and to benefit from other people's. And, as Bruner writes (1996, p 79), *we seem to be more prone to acting our way into thinking than we are able to think our way explicitly into acting.* This is partly why children, especially when grappling with new ideas, require first-hand experience and different ways of representing this (ideas discussed further in Eaude, 2011, pp 117–19).

While children over seven years old are more able to deal with symbolic and abstract ideas than younger ones, they continue to rely heavily on 'learning through doing'. When learning is difficult or insecure, children require the 'earlier' – enactive and iconic – means of representation more, and for longer, than adults tend to recognise. Their teachers should not rely only on language and conscious processes, though they must help and support children to articulate their ideas and learning processes. So, primary classrooms should present opportunities for children to act, interact and talk, to move, explore and create, not just to sit and listen.

Being cared-for and caring-for

Those who work with very young children recognise their need to be cared-for. This does not stop at some mysterious point. We all continue to require this, especially when uncertain or distressed. Noddings (2003) emphasises that each person (whatever their age and status) is at different times the one-caring and the cared-for, seeing these as the foundations of social and moral development; and that each of us benefits from both of these. Moreover, she suggests that people have a biological need to be cared-for and to care for other people and sentient beings. This helps to develop empathy – the ability to see the world from another perspective. Nussbaum argues that empathy is a necessary element of morality since *it is easier to treat people as objects to be manipulated if you have never learned any other way to see them* (2010, p 23); and that the development of empathy does not come naturally but requires imagination, emphasising the role of the humanities in this. However, those who have not been well cared-for may find it difficult, even risky, to care for others and so require the support of caring adults to do so.

Caring-for children does not mean that children should be allowed to act and interact as they wish. Nor does it imply that education is just about children being happy, though it usually helps when they are. Far from it. But it does involve recognising that some children require more support than others if their cognitive processes are not to be overwhelmed by anxiety; and that all children at times need both to be cared-for and to care for others.

The power of example

Young children learn a great deal by example and by imitation, reinforced by practice, though how they develop will depend on what they practise. Children are likely to be more reflective or resourceful if adults model, allow and encourage this; and if they are always expected to conform, will (generally) learn to do so, but at a cost in creativity or lateral thinking. This applies to how children are expected to conduct themselves, from aspects as (apparently) simple as how one responds when annoyed to more complex ones like how to balance honesty and loyalty when a friend does something wrong. It refers to how children learn to build, or sustain, qualities such as persistence or confidence, imagination or criticality. And, in academic subjects, it involves children learning, by watching and practising, how to work as a scientist or an artist, a designer or a historian, building up the procedural knowledge and the ways of working associated with each. So, how trusted adults model actions, attitudes and values is fundamental in what, and how, young children learn.

Inclusive learning environments

The environment – emotional and social as well as physical – influences how we act, encouraging or discouraging particular ways of acting or thinking. Whether in a church, a club or a classroom, we tend to behave like other people there. Interactions with other children, adults and the immediate environment affect both what, and how, an individual child, and a whole class, learns – one reason why assessment of mood is such a vital element of teacher expertise.

The environment and expectations embedded in it exert an influence over time, as children get used to 'small steps' such as saying please and thank you, working together and standing up for themselves, practising their reading and remembering to bring their swimming costume. This helps to build up 'habits of mind', which, Vygotsky argued, are contagious (see Claxton, 2007, p 118). Teachers who encourage such small steps (and many similar habits) matter particularly for young children, given their impressionability and the length of time they spend in one class, with one teacher.

Openness, boundaries and space

While learning tends to be viewed as like climbing a mountain or winning a race, it can also be seen as like visiting (and revisiting) the pictures in a gallery or the exhibits in a museum. Palmer (1983, 1993, pp 71–75) suggests that an authentic learning space has three essential dimensions: *openness, boundaries and an air of hospitality*. He sees the openness of a space as involving a lack of clutter and *created by the firmness of its boundaries*, a structure for learning, not *an invitation to confusion and chaos* (p 72). Boundaries, such as rules and routines, help young children, especially, by containing the anxiety of too great a choice, but if too tight can constrain their creativity. Openness enables children to take more control of their learning, but runs the risk of them only choosing to do what is familiar, unfocussed or unchallenging.

Learning involves challenge, but children (and we all), at times, especially when life is tough, require what Kimes Myers (1997, p 63) calls 'hospitable space', a haven – the chance to play, to reflect, to experiment, to imagine. Sometimes, young children benefit from activities being pacy, for example, in mental maths or completing a presentation; at others, they need space, to design a model, to solve a problem. Or just to enjoy the beauty of an autumn leaf or reflect on what is troubling them.

Ready, willing and able

Claxton (2007) emphasises the need to broaden, strengthen and deepen qualities, attributes and dispositions, so that children can apply them in an increasingly wide and challenging range of situations, with greater depth and sophistication. He compares learning to strengthening muscles by regular exercise. Claxton and Carr (2004, p 87) write, *we have tended to articulate these goals in terms of a combination of learning inclinations, sensitivities to occasion, and skills. We have described them as being ready, willing and able to engage profitably with learning.* It is not enough for children to be able to act in particular ways – such as saying their tables or using a search engine – if they are not ready or willing to do so. Children acquire and embed skills mainly by using them; and if children are unable to achieve their goals, they require practice and support to use their skills so that increasingly they can.

Claxton and Carr (2004) categorise learning environments as prohibiting, affording, inviting or potentiating. They present potentiating learning environments as *those that not only invite the expression of certain dispositions, but actively 'stretch' them, and thus develop them. It is our view that potentiating environments involve frequent participation in shared activity … in which children or students take responsibility for directing those activities, as well as adults* (pp 91–92). Unless young children are engaged and active, applying skills in contexts and activities that matter to them, a significant proportion are unlikely to be included or have their 'learning muscles' exercised.

Breadth and balance

A healthy body requires a balanced diet. This does not mean everyone should eat the same, but each person needs variety. The same is true of the development of the whole child. Children need, and have the legal right to, a broad and balanced curriculum, providing different routes into learning. They thrive on a diet rich in activity and reflection, in stories and silences, in drama and poetry, in music and design, in play and in playfulness, in challenges to be overcome and opportunities to be explored; and in talk to develop the deep learning and processes of enquiry common to many subject areas. In Alexander's words (1992, p 141), *curriculum breadth and balance are less about time allocation than the diversity of challenge of what the child encounters.*

One reason why a broad curriculum benefits young children is that each child has several parallel developmental trajectories in which progress takes place at different rates. So, a child's reading may develop rapidly, although his physical development is delayed by poor gross motor skills; and her mathematical abilities and confidence may be less than those in music or drama or her social skills. Success in one area often leads to the confidence which encourages engagement in others. A second reason is that young children often make unusual connections, across subject boundaries, especially when encouraged to do so, or not inhibited from doing so. Some may not lead anywhere, but others may open up new possibilities or link apparently unconnected ideas.

A third reason is that a broad range of experiences can help uncover hidden talents or develop new interests, which if children are not encouraged to try they, and others, will not know about. The fourth, possibly most important, reason is that, as a succession of reports (summarised in Alexander, 2010, chapter 3) indicate, a relentless focus on literacy and numeracy is unlikely to be the best route to achieve high standards and engagement in the long term in these. So, breadth and balance is a vital element of an inclusive classroom environment for young children.

The dynamics of the primary classroom

Classrooms are complex places, not just because of how those in any group together for a long time interact, but because of the dynamics within the group. Jackson (1968, p 10) identifies three aspects of the hidden curriculum – the implicit aspects of how a classroom works – which strongly influence how children respond:

» crowds;

» praise; and

» power.

Crowds, praise and power

The primary classteacher has the challenge of trying to meet individual needs while catering for those of the whole group. The effect of being in a crowd is most obvious for very young children. Whereas, out of school, they can usually speak when they want, they are, in a class of up to 30 children, expected to wait, at the age when they may want to be noticed. Of course, this is part of learning to regulate one's immediate desires and to take turns, but it can easily lead to children becoming passive and disengaged from learning, or disruptive. It is easy to become anonymous in the crowd; or to gain attention by standing out from it.

While teaching a class of young children can be very enjoyable, it often leads to the teacher feeling isolated, despite all the busy-ness, and worried about losing control. Young children's responses tend to be more volatile and less predictable than those of older children, since they find self-regulation more difficult, especially when in a group. For example, a silly noise or pulling a face may prompt others to follow suit, usually to the amusement of everyone except the teacher. Children's conduct is strongly influenced by the reactions of others. However, usually, they are most easily influenced by an adult pointing out those who do behave appropriately. So the classteacher must be skilled in interacting with the group, without wasting time and energy, if children are to be active and on-task.

Classroom life involves constant evaluation and competition with others. This is not just formally through tests, but through subtler processes such as which reading book a child is given, which group she is allocated to and whose contributions are taken notice of. People and groups are motivated by different things: money, fame, duty, competition, fear, enjoyment, approval, praise. You can think of more, I am sure. As discussed further in Chapter 5, young children tend to respond well to praise and being encouraged to do better than they did previously. However, as Alexander (1995, p 206) writes, *praise may not be what it seems. For one thing, it becomes devalued if it is used too often and without discrimination; for another the use of overt praise may be at variance with other messages about children's work which a teacher is conveying and which children readily pick up.* And while competition with others can help to spur some children on (as it did for me), it does not operate the same for every group. In Brantlinger's (2003, p 13) words, *because [working class and lower income families] rarely benefit from it, the competitive school structure does not play the same motivating role for them as for middle class students. Class advantage may be invisible to those who benefit, but subordinates are acutely aware of barriers to opportunity.* Those of you who are women, or from ethnic minorities, may understand the existence of such invisible barriers more easily; but all teachers must seek to overcome them if their classrooms are to be inclusive.

So, schools are not 'level playing fields', not only because of children's previous experience, and which types of knowledge or experience are most valued, but the way in which many practices taken for granted in the classroom operate. As a result, many children, mainly but not exclusively from ethnic minorities and socio-economically disadvantaged backgrounds, may regard school as not for them. The self-esteem and motivation of a child made to feel that she is 'not-good-enough' is likely to be diminished; and when this is repeated such children may feel written off and become disengaged.

It might appear that, in the classroom, the teacher exerts considerable power. In some respects, this is so, since the teacher can, to a considerable extent, determine activities, reward appropriate behaviour and punish what is not. However, individuals and groups of children have more power to determine what happens in the classroom and influence the teacher than is commonly recognised. This is a major factor in why teachers find relinquishing control so risky, despite appearing to be powerful.

How young children and their teachers affect each other

Cooper and McIntyre (1996, pp 116–18) emphasise what they call bi-directionality – where teachers' strategies and behaviours influence, and are influenced by, pupils'. For example, children may feel uncertain when teachers expect them to do what is unfamiliar and challenging, and Pollard (1985) identified many occasions where pupils behaved well in return for relatively undemanding tasks, describing this as a working consensus. So there is a subtle pressure to set low-level work where children achieve success but their learning is not extended.

As well as being physically exhausting, teaching a class of young children often evokes in the teacher strong emotional responses. I recall, as most teachers can, particular children who managed to get 'under my skin', provoking me to inappropriate responses, so that I made a situation worse by focusing on their poor behaviour, or becoming exasperated, in front of the whole class. Kimes Myers (1997, p 8), drawing on Erikson's work, describes this as cog-wheeling, writing that *when we engage in relationship with young children … the child within us also has a developing edge.* So, the adult–child relationship is not a one-way process. Primary classteachers must be aware how particular actions and individuals can provoke in them strong emotional responses which affect their own actions; and be prepared to modify their own behaviours rather than always expect children to alter theirs.

The effect of how primary classteachers teach

As Berliner (2001, p 465) writes, *policies from the principals, superintendents and school board … along with expectations of the community, determine the organization of a school and its climate. These policies subtly but powerfully, affect teachers' attitudes, beliefs, enthusiasms, sense of efficacy, conception of their responsibilities, and teaching practices.* When combined with more feelings such as a sense of isolation, worry about one's own abilities or an uncertainty about professional identity, external factors, such as the pressure to achieve results quickly, to cover a large amount of content or to teach in a particular way, affect how teachers act and think.

As the Cambridge Primary Review (Alexander, 2010, especially chapter 14) argues, it has proved hard, if not impossible, to shake off the idea that educating young children is about what he calls Curriculum 1 (often called 'the basics') at the expense of Curriculum 2 (aspects such as the humanities and the expressive arts), despite how the latter help to shape identity. The current emphasis on the standards agenda assumes that success is measured largely by attainment in tests of literacy and numeracy. This exerts a strong influence on teachers' priorities and how they teach, especially when linked to high-stakes assessment. In particular, the emphasis on measurable outcomes in English and maths makes it extremely difficult for headteachers and teachers working in areas where levels of attainment are low, often socio-economically disadvantaged areas, to provide breadth, balance and richness of experience. So, those children who most need a broad and balanced curriculum because their experience outside school limits the horizons of possibility too often receive a limited diet.

It is understandable that policy-makers should wish to measure outcomes, to monitor and inspect teaching and to decide what material teachers should cover. The difficulty is that these alter how teachers act and how they see their role. So, while measurable outcomes in reading or mathematics may help teachers and parents/carers to assess children's progress, using these as the main basis for judging success leads to other subject areas being marginalised. Inspection and monitoring can help to identify strengths and weaknesses, but encourage teachers to adapt their teaching to meet what they think the observer will want, and not seeing or taking unexpected opportunities. And while a curriculum can help to ensure entitlement, it tends, if set out in great detail, to encourage teachers to cover a large amount of content, resulting in superficial learning (of facts) rather than deep learning (of concepts). The more prominence is given to these, and the higher the stakes, the more likely they are to encourage compliance. This is, presumably, the intention, but such pressures influence how teachers understand their role and reduce their autonomy and discourage principled performance, two key characteristics of professionalism.

The effect on primary classteachers' attitudes and beliefs

One cumulative effect of processes such as target-setting, data gathering, detailed planning and monitoring is not only to make teachers too busy to be reflective, but to create a sense of fearfulness and being not good enough. This undermines the confidence which enables and encourages intuition and improvisation. Such confidence derives largely from self-belief, which comes in part from experience, in part from a depth of knowledge about teaching, about the context, about that particular class of children.

These pressures lead to teachers being anxious about — and wishing to over-control — children's behaviour and to be defensive and adopt safe but uncreative approaches where they feel comfortable but which limit opportunities for children's learning. This means that many classteachers are likely to adopt transmissive, teacher-dominated, styles of teaching, the limitations of which are discussed in Chapter 5; and may have little incentive to let children dwell on issues which require extensive thought, or to spend much time on the humanities and the arts.

It is natural for teachers to want to simplify, but fear of loss of control easily leads to oversimplification, where children are praised for compliance rather than creativity; and where teachers place more emphasis on outcomes than processes, on cognitive than emotional aspects of learning, rather than seeing how these are intimately intertwined. Such responses matter not only for teachers, but for children, because, as Alexander (2010, p 496) argues, *pupils will not learn to think for themselves if their teachers are expected merely to do as they are told.* And too much adult control tends to make children's behaviour dependent on reward and punishment rather than intrinsic motivation.

Nias (1989, pp 196–97), in her study of how primary school teachers understand their work, suggests that:

the very nature of teaching, as [these teachers] experience it, is contradictory. Teachers must nurture the whole while attending to the parts, liberate their pupils to grow in some directions by checking growth in others, foster and encourage progress by controlling it and show love and interest by curbing and chastising … My claim is … that to adopt the identity of an English primary school teacher is to accept the paradoxical nature of the task and inexorably to live with tension.

Nias argued that primary teachers were strongly influenced by beliefs about the aims of education and the nature of young children which led to a close association between their personal and professional identities. As a result of this and their reluctance to say no, primary classteachers may be influenced by external pressures more strongly than those in other phases not only in how they teach but in aspects such as confidence and morale. The emphasis on results and curriculum coverage exerts particularly strong pressure to focus on these when working with nine and ten year-olds. But classteachers with a high level of expertise manage, like all experts, to address external expectations while quietly taking account of broader aims.

The role of the primary classteacher beyond the classroom

We tend to assume that one classteacher teaches a class of primary-age children for almost all subjects most of the week for one year; and that the group remains the same for much of the week. Increasingly, this may no longer be so, at least in England. For example, the introduction of planning, preparation and assessment (PPA) time means that the class is taught by at least one other adult – not always a teacher – for at least 10 per cent of the week, often in subjects such as music, art and physical education; and, especially with ten and 11 year-olds, many schools split up classes for some subjects, notably maths and sometimes English and science. Moreover, there are likely to be several support staff, including teaching assistants, working within the classroom or with small groups in intervention programmes with particular groups of children, such as those with English as an additional language or special educational needs.

The number of adults may have benefits, for instance in providing greater expertise in one subject area or additional support for children or groups with particular needs. However, it may lead to the classteacher being mainly responsible for literacy and numeracy, rather than the whole curriculum; and mean that only for relatively short periods of time in any week does the classteacher have the whole class together. This makes it harder for her to have an overview of 'the whole child', to make links between subject areas and to develop her knowledge of, and expertise in teaching, some subjects. As a result, the classteacher may find that she teaches only part of the curriculum and becomes more like a manager of learning, liaising with and overseeing several adults.

Primary classteachers do not only work directly with children. They will be expected to spend a considerable time on recording and analysing data, record-keeping and writing plans or reports. They will probably have to liaise with other colleagues in the school in aspects such as planning the curriculum and school events from the Harvest Festival to an artist in residence, from swimming to arranging a residential trip; and with those outside the school to support individual children with specific health, cognitive or behavioural needs or to ensure that outside agencies are called in if need be. These demands can often seem burdensome, or even overwhelming.

Classteachers have a responsibility to liaise formally with parents/carers through parent consultations and reports and often do so more informally. This requires different facets of expertise, for instance in:

> explaining how children are progressing and the reasons for, and benefits of, particular approaches to teaching;

> encouraging some parents/carers not to exert too much pressure on their children and others to provide more support; or

> ensuring that children whose parents may be reluctant for them to go on school trips are encouraged and supported to do so.

As with children, parents/carers bring different experiences, expectations and attitudes towards school – and the classteacher has to judge when, and how, to include, to involve or sometimes to challenge them.

IN A **NUTSHELL**

This chapter has argued that meeting multiple aims for a wide range of children, over time, makes the primary classteacher's role particularly demanding. The social and emotional dynamics in the classroom, the scope of the role and external expectations can easily combine to undermine classteachers' sense of agency and confidence. This often leads to a wish to oversimplify and to control and so not to adopt the full repertoire of pedagogies most likely to enhance children's learning. So, in Chapter 5, we consider how teachers with a high level of expertise in teaching a class of young children act and think, in the light of these influences.

REFLECTIONS ON **CRITICAL ISSUES**

- *Primary classteachers have to meet a range of aims broader, and often more contradictory, than those of other teachers.*
- *Young children's learning is affected by their dependence on relationships of trust, their need for active learning and the power of example.*
- *How classrooms operate makes it hard for all children to be included, especially those whose experience is often not valued most highly.*
- *The volatility, range of personalities and the social dynamics of a class of young children and external expectations makes it very demanding to make appropriate provision for all children's learning needs.*
- *External expectations exert a strong influence on primary classteachers' confidence and identity and how they think and act, tending to make them cautious.*

CRITICAL ISSUES

- *What types of teacher knowledge are most important for primary classteachers?*
- *What sorts of objectives should be set and feedback provided?*
- *How do primary classteachers with a high level of expertise understand and respond to unexpected events?*
- *How do primary classteachers create and sustain a climate for learning which encourages active learning?*
- *What attitudes and beliefs do primary classteachers with a high level of expertise hold?*

Introduction

The simple answer to the question posed in the title of this book is that primary classteachers with a high level of expertise all act somewhat differently, because the context is always unpredictable. Teachers are pragmatic. Classteachers make the classroom work, taking into account the dilemmas inherent in teaching a class. Those with a high level of expertise with young children understand how they learn, recognise the dilemmas and organise the classroom accordingly.

The length of time which young children spend with one teacher, their need for care and adult support and the breadth of what is to be achieved means that primary classteachers must be more like decathletes, very good at several events at once, than sprinters or high jumpers, brilliant at only one discipline. But they are well placed to help children to make links and connections across different areas of their lives because they teach different subject areas and for longer. For example, rhythms in music can be linked to patterns in mathematics; and children's writing may be enhanced by using their knowledge of new technologies. This is part of the joy, as well as the challenge, of the role.

This chapter returns to the key areas of teacher expertise set out on pages 19–20 and summarised in the questions above. The first half explores different types of teacher knowledge which classteachers of young children require, with domain, craft and personal/ interpersonal knowledge all closely interlinked. The second half considers climate and context, approaches to teaching and attitudes and beliefs. This leads towards 12 tentative propositions about how classteachers with a high level of expertise with young children act and think. These are designed to prompt debate, since the prototypical nature of expertise means that there is no one template to be followed.

Pedagogical content knowledge

Chapter 3 highlighted Shulman's term pedagogical content knowledge as *the ways of formulating the subject that make it comprehensible to others.* So, while teaching expertise involves being able to present *deep representations of the subject matter*, considerable subject expertise may help, but may be a barrier unless matched with an understanding of how young children learn and why some find it difficult to grasp concepts. The importance of tasks being within what Vygotsky (1978) called the Zone of Proximal Development – just, but not too far, beyond the learners' current level of understanding, between current abilities and possible independent action – means that expertise in teaching is manifested in the level of match between the child's current level of understanding and the challenge provided. Teachers who understand the difficulties that children encounter may be those best positioned to help them overcome these. For example, at the risk of oversimplifying, I have always found spelling easy, and was not good at teaching spelling; whereas I struggled to learn mathematical concepts and found, at least partly as a result, that I was able to understand children's problems and so help them resolve them.

Towards the older end of the primary school, it becomes increasingly difficult to provide appropriate challenge in every subject and a greater depth of subject knowledge may be required. This presents a dilemma, whether to use specialists with more specific expertise and risk fragmenting the curriculum, or to rely on the classteacher's relationship with the class and more generic knowledge but retain opportunities to make cross-curricular links. While many children may benefit from being taught by different teachers, others, especially those who are less confident, may find it hard when the continuity of the relationship with the classteacher is lost.

Black et al. (2002, pp 15–16) suggest that *a high level of subject qualification is less important than a thorough understanding of the fundamental principles of the subject, an understanding of the kinds of difficulties that pupils might have, and the creativity to think up questions that can stimulate productive thinking ... Such pedagogical content knowledge is essential in interpreting responses – what pupils say will contain clues to aspects of their thinking ... but picking up on these requires a thorough knowledge of common difficulties in learning the subject,* continuing that these vary between subjects.

My sense is that, in some subject areas, most obviously music and modern foreign languages, content and procedural knowledge are so intertwined that few classteachers without specialist knowledge in these areas are likely to have enough expertise to teach these well. But in most others the classteacher can gain enough content, conceptual and procedural knowledge, especially where children are encouraged to take more control of their learning. In this case, the teacher's role becomes more to facilitate, guide and support; and expertise is manifested in how questions are asked, dialogue enabled and ways of working encouraged. However, this aspect is undoubtedly one of the more demanding challenges of the primary classteacher's role.

Setting objectives and providing feedback

The idea of pedagogical content knowledge re-emphasises that setting appropriate objectives and providing formative feedback are among the key features of teacher expertise. Unless activities are challenging, young children soon become bored, but if they are unachievable most become demotivated. Unless young children see the point of an activity and are given feedback on what they might do next, they are less likely to be engaged and motivated to use a wide range of learning strategies.

Differing types of objective and means of assessment

Assessment of children's current understanding, and especially assessment-in-the-moment, is a vital aspect of teacher expertise. Since younger children may find it hard to articulate their thought processes, it becomes especially important to draw on a wide range, and various sources, of information. As tests are less reliable with younger children, one should be cautious about the results and ensure that assessment takes place over time, with a range of different techniques and views. For example, with young bilingual learners, it is easy to confuse lack of fluency in English with poor cognitive ability – or (though less frequently) to think that progress is slower because of linguistic rather than cognitive difficulties. In the first case, this can result in grouping those children within 'lower-ability' groups, so reducing the cognitive level and creating low expectations; while in the latter the necessary support may be delayed. So, teachers with a high level of expertise draw on the expertise of others, such as parents/carers and bilingual staff, to form hypotheses about children's learning and how best to enhance it.

Black and Wiliam (1998) emphasise the value of formative assessment, suggesting that this involves a series of practices, many of which are hard to develop and sustain, including:

> » involving pupils in their learning;
> » sharing criteria about what is to be learned and what success would look like; and
> » giving children timely feedback about the quality of work and how to improve (see Eaude, 2011, pp 145–48, for further discussion of formative assessment).

Teachers of young children are often encouraged to use extrinsic rewards, such as stickers and treats. These may motivate some children in the short term, especially those who find it hardest to regulate their emotions. But they tend to lead to good behaviour becoming dependent on such rewards, rather than relying on and developing intrinsic motivation. Intrinsic motivation comes from a sense of autonomy, mastery and purpose – and so is often associated with engagement in, and enjoyment of, activities, from science to sewing, from music to mathematics, from reading to running, where children set their own objectives.

Children benefit from knowing what to do to improve. But targets – for all their current popularity – are too often used to label and to limit children, as when different groups are given targets to achieve, based on their perceived ability, so reinforcing, publicly, those who can and those who can't. While it is often helpful for adults to identify learning objectives, teachers with a high level of expertise help children to set their own goals and apply their skills, rather than just work towards short-term, teacher-determined learning objectives. In particular, they encourage children to develop the qualities associated with successful learners, both in general and increasingly in specific disciplines.

Claxton (2002), in considering how to build children's learning power, argues for transferable qualities such as those he calls the 4Rs:

- » resilience;
- » reciprocity;
- » resourcefulness; and
- » reflectiveness.

These are required in most areas of learning. I would add other qualities such as confidence and co-operation; and values such as honesty, respect and courage. If children are to learn not only to be brave or trusting, but how brave or trusting to be, and how to judge what to do when values clash, they need adults to help them explore this, rather than offer over-simple solutions to such dilemmas. If children are over-protected and too accustomed to easy success, they do not develop the resilience to cope with adversity, difficulty and complexity. While they benefit from predictable relationships, young children have to learn to cope with change and uncertainty. They require opportunities to take risks, make mistakes and find how to overcome difficulties, with support where necessary; and their teachers should not over-protect them, but encourage them to explore and make mistakes, as doors to new learning.

So, teachers with a high level of expertise set not only performance objectives, but those based on learning behaviours; and they make these integral to activities – such as ensuring that teamwork is essential to complete a collaborative task – making explicit what is expected and praising children who achieve these. Claxton's (2007, p 122) idea of split-screen thinking: *maintaining a dual focus on the content of the lesson and the learning dispositions that are currently being expanded* provides a practical way of thinking about this.

Feedback

Teachers with a high level of expertise recognise that feedback takes many forms and is constant, evident in every aspect of the learning environment. For young children, the relationship with, and desire for approval from, trusted adults is a strong motivator. With young children, you tend to 'get more of what you concentrate on'. So, young children usually respond better to praise and to good behaviour being pointed out than to reprimand. But as they approach adolescence, the approval of other children and the impact of cultural influences such as music, magazines and the media become increasingly significant; and being praised in public may become a source of embarrassment rather than motivation.

The less a child can think abstractly, the more immediate and specific feedback needs to be. Spoken feedback, either individually or as a group, to point out straightaway what children have done well and what to work on, is more useful than written marks and grades; as is praise for adopting good learning behaviours, such as remembering to plan before starting or to label a graph or for showing kindness, self-control or co-operation. Constant praise is of little value and, as Dweck (2000) argues, when linked to intelligence, leads to children becoming brittle and unresilient.

While feedback is usually associated with comments by adults, children benefit from learning to assess their own, and each other's, work. This is difficult and takes time to learn, but teachers with a high level of expertise help and expect children, from a young age, to identify for themselves what they are doing well and how to improve; and for groups to do so, honestly but supportively, for each other – all of which requires an environment for learning where there is collaboration and trust. Mayall (2010, pp 67–68) suggests that learning communities which are collaborative and within which children are valued and value each other lead to children being happier and to academic results improving, reflecting the social nature of learning and that mutual respect is a prerequisite for learning.

Understanding and responding to events

Classteachers with a high level of expertise with young children are attuned both to individual children and to the whole class. Because young children tend to respond more immediately and intensely to events which excite, animate or disturb them, assessment of the mood of a class is a vital aspect of expertise in teaching them. A class may seem lively or sluggish, animated or fractious. Understanding this enables the teacher to change direction or activity from that planned, or to extend a discussion in which children are particularly engaged; and emphasises the significance of timing. Miss the chance and it may not come again. Hold off too long and the class may be disrupted. Intervene too quickly and one may stop a child or the class from thinking in depth.

Classteachers with a high level of expertise use subtle, often intuitive, types of cue-interpretation and assessment to decide how best to adapt their planning. They are more able, and quicker, to recognise not just cognitive, but emotional and behavioural, cues, and to notice and exploit unexpected or original ideas – in part because they pay attention to children's responses. For example, a child's comment or question may steer discussion into interesting areas, help to make a good link, or demonstrate a conceptual misunderstanding; and a small fracas between children may indicate an unresolved incident or just a temporary falling-out. Such cues help teachers to formulate hypotheses about an individual's learning and possibly identify areas where several children may share the same misunderstanding. This is a further reason to encourage children's questions and attend to their answers. On one occasion, at the end of what I had thought a very good lesson on volcanoes, I asked if the children had any final questions. Jane tentatively put her hand up and asked, 'But why do people make volcanoes?' Maybe, not such a good lesson! As Shulman (2004, p 413) advises, *you must respect the intelligence and understanding of students especially when they misunderstand.*

As indicated in Chapter 2, more frequent testing of hypotheses (not of children) is one key feature of expertise, to check that hunches match with new information. For instance, it is easy, even when one knows a class well, to pitch a lesson at too simple or challenging a level. Teachers with a high level of expertise do not maintain a slavish adherence to learning objectives, but are prepared to change tack, to create, to see and to take opportunities, especially with young children. This does not mean that there is no need to plan; rather that planning should be sufficiently flexible to allow for in-the-moment judgements to respond to unpredictable challenges and opportunities.

Creating opportunities may involve giving the class the chance to experiment with different ways of formulating or approaching a problem, rather than saying how it should be done. Seeing opportunities may result from the comment or actions of one individual or group, indicating a particularly interesting way of approaching a task, or that the activity, as planned, is too advanced or too simple. Taking opportunities may consist of having the insight, and often the courage, to risk departing from what is planned, or adapting a lesson in the light of such events. You may wish to ponder on opportunities you have created, seen and taken; and others where you failed to do so. I remember discovering by chance, or rather by noticing, an eight year-old with an extensive knowledge of geology and two 11 year-olds who were wonderful disco dancers, though I never capitalised on either as I should have.

Leading a class discussion – a case study

Let us take the example of a class discussion. As Meier writes (cited in Shulman, 2004, p 485), *the essence of learning is telling and the essence of teaching is listening.* Children's talk is an essential part of constructing knowledge. To rehearse to oneself often helps to clarify one's thinking. To explain to others often helps to understand and extend a child's own thinking more deeply. Yet schools too often expect children to learn passively, by listening, from knowledge transmitted by the teacher. Since young children, especially, may need time to gather their thoughts, or find it hard to talk in front of a whole class, teachers with a high level of expertise often encourage them to talk to each other in pairs or small groups rather than expecting instant answers. They draw out the reluctant speaker – and (gently) keep in check those who speak too much. Such teachers question, or prompt, or commentate (see Claxton and Carr, 2004) or reframe or elaborate children's ideas, but they encourage and let children do the thinking, rather than do it for them. So, they wait rather than answer their own questions, and suggest alternatives or exceptions to challenge children's current understanding. Above all, they see classroom talk as dialogue, rather than a one-way monologue.

Climate and context

Creating and sustaining the climate and conditions for learning and greater respect for a wide range of personalities, backgrounds and aptitudes have been highlighted as central aspects of teacher expertise, not least because the teacher has considerable influence on these.

Creating an inclusive classroom environment is not simply about providing for children of different backgrounds or ensuring that equipment or the curriculum is adapted for those with special educational needs. It involves what Mayall (2010, p 66) calls the 'moral order of the school'. This is much more than the teacher telling children what is right and wrong – if only teaching were so simple! It entails creating a structure where particular ways of acting and interacting are expected – and others challenged. For instance, where similarities and differences between people are celebrated and where respect for each other's differences – of background, language, religion and abilities – is expected, and racism, bullying and other forms of unkindness are not accepted. Take the example of bullying. Teachers with a high level of expertise do not just protect children who are bullied, but help those bullied to devise and apply strategies to respond to bullies; and bullies to understand the impact of their actions. They are prepared to raise, and respond to, difficult issues, both proactively where need be and in response to particular incidents or questions; and they make judgements about how best to do so and whether individually or as a group.

The key areas of teacher expertise on pages 19–20 were described as particularly benefiting younger children and those from disadvantaged backgrounds. Teachers with a high level of expertise search out, show respect for, and draw on, the knowledge and interests of all children, especially those who may be reluctant to share these; and where appropriate adapt how they teach. For instance, I recall several children becoming far more animated when asked about their own culture, religion or interests; and many who became much more engaged when given practical tasks associated with what they understood from experience out of school. As the TLRP suggested on page 4, *the conception of what is to be learned needs to be broadened beyond the notions of curricula and subjects associated with schools.*

Primary classteachers with a high level of expertise recognise that children's engagement and responses depend on a wide range of factors – relationships, trust, the activities, the classroom climate and children's prior experience and the emotions resulting from what they (and their teachers) have experienced out of school. So, they rely on relationship more than reprimand or reward and avoid taking (too much) advantage of young children's tendency to accept implicitly what the teacher says. Such teachers influence behaviour in subtle ways, such as pointing out when other children conduct themselves appropriately or challenging what is inappropriate with a gesture or a look. But they recognise that learning must be reciprocal and that what benefits some children may not be what the whole class needs; and so they balance predictability and sensitivity with individual need, structure with freedom, pace with space, challenge with haven, over time. They make expectations – and the reasons for them – explicit and reinforce and model what these entail not just in specific lessons, but throughout the curriculum, formal, informal and hidden.

A repertoire of pedagogies

The classteacher is key to how the learning environment is created and sustained. Those with a high level of expertise seek to meet long-term as well as short-term goals. For young children, in particular, this requires an extensive repertoire of pedagogies. What is appropriate will vary according to the children's age, the subject being taught, the mood of the class and above all what the teacher seeks to achieve. So, remembering how aims, styles of teaching and the fabric of pedagogy are all linked, classteachers working with young children must try to ensure that these are all aligned. For example, it is no use planning a discussion and ignoring children's comments; or asking children to co-operate but not giving them the chance to work together and think how best to do so.

The limitations of transmission

Alexander (2008, p 36) highlights two main styles of teaching: *didactic*, where the teacher is largely in control, and *exploratory*, which places the learner centre-stage. Unless children exercise some control over their learning, they are likely to become passive learners. Some tasks require more direction, others less, but teachers with a high level of expertise look to hand over control to children, where possible, following their interests and lines of thought. This involves remaining in control, but without being controlling, and tending towards styles of teaching where children are 'co-agents' in their own learning – involved in the planning of activities and how these are carried out.

Alexander (2008, pp 78–81), discussing different versions of teaching, such as transmission, negotiation and facilitation, indicates that each may be valuable for encouraging different types of learning, with some emphasised more, or less, in different cultures and systems. However, he argues that transmission is inappropriate as the main strategy, especially for young children, not least because it reduces the opportunities for reflective, deeper understanding. As Desforges (1995, p 129) suggests, *[direct instruction] is never, on its own, sufficient to ensure deeper understanding, problem solving, creativity, or group work capacities.* And in Katz's words (2003, p 368), *when formal instruction is introduced too early, too intensely and too abstractly, the children may indeed learn the instructed knowledge and skills, but they may do so at the expense of the disposition to use them.* So, earlier is not better, especially if children are not engaged or do not have the disposition to learn; and while common sense may suggest that a focus on results and outcomes is the best route into learning, this may often not be so. Think, for instance, how puppets, or drama, or stories, can enable a class to understand and internalise a message better than direct instruction; or how making drinks may be the best way to learn about capacity, or writing about an exciting activity can help to overcome a reluctant writer's inhibitions.

An apprenticeship approach

Classteachers with a high level of expertise recognise how their own thinking and actions help to shape children's ideas and responses. The importance of example and role-modelling for young children emphasises the value of an apprenticeship approach. This term is used by Gardner (1993) and Rogoff (1990), who also writes of 'guided participation', to describe an approach where children learn from watching and practising alongside adults who model, for instance, how to:

» act and interact, dealing with different situations and emotions, exemplifying values and ways of living;

» approach learning, both in general and as a mathematician, or an artist, or a geographer; and

» use and develop qualities and attributes, both obvious ones like trustworthiness and persistence, but less easy ones (for teachers) like curiosity and imagination.

Without this, young children, especially, are unlikely to develop these qualities.

An apprenticeship approach may seem rather daunting, but no teacher can avoid modelling a set of beliefs and values. Since much of classroom life involves ordinary actions and interactions, these are often manifested in small, apparently trivial, actions. Except that they are not trivial. Jackson et al. (1993, pp 286–87) write that the teachers in their study of the moral life of classrooms did not use the term 'role model' much, suggesting that this may be because it seems too 'heroic'. They spoke of 'humbler virtues' such as:

» showing respect for others;

» demonstrating what it means to be intellectually absorbed;

» paying close attention to what is being said;

» being a 'good sport'; and even

» showing that it is OK to make mistakes and to be confused.

These are integral to how classteachers actually operate, though the pace of classroom life may leave little space for intellectual absorption or really paying close attention to children's responses; and the pressure for results may discourage teachers from taking risks or appearing confused.

Since young children tend to assume that teachers are all-knowing, or at least learn to defer to what they say, teachers working with young children should be slightly wary of appearing too confident, even though confidence is a key feature of expertise. If children are to learn to be critical of what they hear or read, their teachers should not show too much certainty – and should be prepared to be challenged. Children's questions often help to identify conceptual errors or offer other children alternative ways of thinking about or approaching a problem. They can also encourage teachers to make explicit their own thinking processes or ways of acting or to use alternative means of explanation. So teachers with a high level of expertise are assured in how they teach, but may display uncertainty, or refrain from being too authoritative, to encourage children to challenge their authority and think for themselves. This is captured in Claxton's (1997) reference to 'confident uncertainty', an ability to tolerate ambiguity, leaving space for uncertainty and the unknown, which he sees as integral to creative teaching.

Often overlooked are qualities such as humour and enthusiasm. Young children love teachers to use humour or to be silly, as long as the humour is not directed at children and the children understand that the silliness is not serious. Jokes, puns, eccentricity, moving out of role will often be part of the repertoire of the classteacher working with young children. And we probably all remember a teacher whose enthusiasm inspired us. A teacher's genuine enthusiasm can be very motivating. For me, it was the man who taught me history when I was between ten and twelve years old, fuelling my interest and imagination. This emphasises the need for authenticity and passion, the belief that teaching, and what and who one is teaching, matter, recalling the link between personal and professional identity.

Reverting to what feels comfortable

It is hard to keep teaching in ways that enhance young children's learning. For instance, Galton et al. (1999, p 112) indicate that research has repeatedly highlighted that teachers use challenging questioning relatively infrequently compared to 'telling' and 'showing', whatever style of teaching is adopted, not only in the UK but in schools throughout the world. While whole-class teaching may be appropriate for passing on information or for discussion, it must be balanced with individual and group work. Yet many research projects (eg Galton et al., 1980, Galton et al., 1999) indicate how rarely children work as a group, rather than just in a group. If they are to learn to work co-operatively, children must be grouped accordingly, even though they may feel more comfortable with their friends. And if grouping is not to confirm perceptions of fixed ability, varied criteria for grouping children are needed.

So, classteachers with a high level of expertise are sensitive to how children are grouped – and differentiate in different ways, such as by task, by outcome, by support or by questioning, according to what they seek to achieve. And they work actively to counter some beliefs about teaching which are deep-rooted in our culture. For example, adults tend to find the image of a teacher talking and of children sitting still and listening appealing. About three years ago I was involved in a project where teachers were observed and filmed teaching a lesson and then discussed with the observing teacher what they could (both) learn – before swapping roles subsequently. With one class, I encouraged them to notice and interpret patterns from a series of graphs, initially all together and then in groups. With another, I gave them the task of designing a pendulum in groups and finding out what happened when the length of the pendulum, or the weight of the bob, changed. Both sessions went well, and it is impossible to know which class learned most. But the more formal session felt (and looked on the video) more convincing because I (the teacher) was more in control, while the other seemed messier, in part because the children were more in control – and were (apparently) not so on-task the whole time. Take a moment to think what style of teaching makes you feel most comfortable as a teacher or as a learner – and whether these are the best methods of enhancing learning.

Attitudes and beliefs

Expertise in teaching a class, especially of young children, is not just a question of strategies and techniques or activities and experiences. It involves holding on to a breadth of aims, over time, and being attuned to how the class is responding to different teaching strategies. In particular, it depends on expectations, attitudes and beliefs about ideas such as standards and curriculum, intelligence and inclusion and how these relate to children's learning. These provide the basis for informed and sensitive 'patterns of resolution' which more consistently enhance all children's learning.

While teachers with a high level of expertise with young children are keen to achieve high standards, their view of standards is much broader than one based only on skills and performance in literacy and numeracy. They enable children not only to read but to become readers; and not just learn to 'do fractions' but to understand when and how this knowledge can and should be applied. They see standards in terms of well-being and character, not just academic subjects. And they recognise that there are many ways to enable children to become literate and numerate and develop the qualities, attitudes and dispositions to become successful learners.

Classteachers with a high level of expertise help children to be able to cope confidently with what is uncertain and new. In Eaude (2011, pp 171–76) I query whether young children are being educated to meet the challenges they will face in a world of rapid, constant, but as yet unforeseen, change. For example, the immediate availability of a huge amount of information seems to imply that gathering and memorising facts should matter less than being able to critique and assess what is valid and relevant. The demands of globalisation make the ability to relate to, and work with, those who are different matter even more than in the past. And the ability to communicate confidently, in speech and through other means, and to use new technologies, will be increasingly vital.

Chapter 3 emphasised the significance of how teachers view intelligence and Chapter 4 that of including the whole range of children. Too often, teachers underestimate what children can do and do not include all children, even when they try to and believe that they do so. Classteachers with a high level of expertise do things like:

» look out for unexpected abilities, especially in children who are not flourishing or easily included;

» recognise how easily children can be excluded by other children, by the curriculum, by teachers' own attitudes and behaviours; and

» realise that children do not just learn what they are taught explicitly and so trust a range of learning processes.

In brief, such teachers act differently, because they think differently.

IN A **NUTSHELL**

Teachers all work differently, but they should take calculated risks. So, let me risk suggesting, tentatively, 12 propositions about classteachers with a high level of expertise with young children. These are that they:

1. are more concerned with a broad range of pedagogical content knowledge and ways of working and thinking within disciplines than just with subject knowledge;

2. seek to match activities and experiences to children's current level of understanding, but allow scope for individuals and groups to adapt these;

3. regard assessment, especially in-the-moment, and disciplined improvisation, rather than planning with predetermined outcomes, as integral to teaching;

4. adopt a range of pedagogies, depending on what is to be learned, but with a strong element of apprenticeship, enabling children to be active and take increasing control of their learning;

5. are attuned to the emotional and cognitive needs, both of individuals and of the whole class, to inform both planning and methods of feedback;

6. create and sustain, over time, an inclusive learning environment sensitive to, and respectful of, children's culture and background, but helping to expand their cultural horizons;

7. provide a broad and challenging range of activities, experiences and opportunities to sustain children's interest and to broaden, strengthen and deepen the skills, attributes and dispositions associated with lifelong learning;

8. encourage risk-taking and creativity, both independently and in groups, but protect children, especially the least resilient, from the emotional cost of failure;

9. seek to understand and influence, rather than control, children's behaviour, recognising the many factors which affect this and the importance of caring relationships;

10. recognise that education involves multiple, and often conflicting, aims and maintain an emphasis on children's long-term needs, helping to encourage intrinsic motivation;

11. believe that every child can achieve more than she or he thinks that they can, and encourage and support them in having and meeting broad as well as high aspirations;

12. have the confidence to make their own professional, and informed, judgements, both long term and in-the-moment, in response to the group's needs, rather than simply to comply.

CHAPTER 6 | CONCLUSION

> *We do not say that opinions, decisions, and outlooks of other [people] count for nothing, or deny that the teacher's freedom to act on what he or she believes and desires may be greatly constrained by both institutional and social forces, some of them emanating from outside the school itself. But we do insist that within such limits teachers must be seen and see themselves as occupying key roles in classrooms – not simply as technicians who know how to run good discussions or teach encoding skills to beginning readers but as persons whose view of life, which includes all that goes on in classrooms, promises to be as influential in the long run as any of their technical skills.*
>
> *(Jackson et al., 1993, p 277)*

Introduction

This book has presented teaching a class of young children as a much more complex task than that set out in the Teachers' Standards or the long tradition, within and beyond the profession, which associates expertise mainly with those who teach older students. You are probably thinking that this has presented an enormously complicated view of teaching and that developing expertise is a daunting prospect. I hope so, because comparisons between teaching and other professions indicated the complexity of teaching and the expertise required to carry it out. Subsequent chapters have suggested that teaching a class of young children is very demanding, because of the multiplicity of aims, the diversity of children's different needs and the breadth of knowledge and qualities required.

Despite this, there are many primary classteachers with a high level of expertise, who appear to be often fairly ordinary and unassuming people but act and think in extraordinary ways, exerting a profound influence on children. This chapter returns to think about those who have different levels of expertise in teaching and offer some tentative pointers for teachers, headteachers and teacher educators towards how expertise can be developed. However, remember that the discussion has necessarily been descriptive not prescriptive – that it tells us about how teachers with a high level of expertise work, but does not offer a blueprint to copy. Expertise in teaching is too complex for that. Developing it requires thought and practice over time.

Key differences between beginning teachers and those with a high level of expertise

One key insight of the Cambridge Primary Review (Alexander 2010, pp 416–18) is that expert teachers seem to act and think in subtly different ways from novices, rather than just doing the same things better, or quicker, or more economically. To explore this, let us look at the box below which summarises the five stages identified on pages 3 and 4 and the types of strategy, approach and characteristic involved.

Strategies, approaches and characteristics in developing teacher expertise

Stage	Strategies	Overall approach	Characteristic
Novice	Context-free rules and guidelines	Relatively inflexible, limited skill	Deliberate
Advanced beginner	Practical case knowledge	Use of rules qualified by greater understanding of conditions	Insightful
Competent	Discrimination of what matters or not	Conscious choices, but not yet fast, fluid or flexible	Rational
Proficient	Accumulated case knowledge enabling key points to be noticed	Degree of intuition based on prediction of pupil response	Intuitive
Expert	Deep reserves of tacit knowledge	Apparently effortless, fluid, instinctive, though able to fall back on deliberate, analytical approach	Arational

(adapted from Alexander, 2010, pp 416–17)

Developing expertise entails moving from a dependence on external rules and guidelines to a reliance on tacit knowledge, accumulating case knowledge to decide on what matters most. In terms of approach, this involves an increasing level of flexibility and fluidity, based on prediction of likely responses and intuition, but with the ability to be more analytic when necessary. Most intriguingly, it calls for moving from acting deliberately and consciously towards relying more on intuition, except when encountering what is beyond one's immediate experience.

Teachers with a high level of expertise make complicated situations easier for themselves and for learners by the use of predictable rules and routines. But they do not restrict children's learning by oversimplifying tasks and experiences, recognising the complexity and variety of different children's learning processes. They enable and encourage different routes, both conscious and unconscious, into learning. While simplifying teaching strategies makes teaching easier, and is necessary at times, it is less likely to develop deep learning for either the child or the teacher.

In Schwab's words (cited in Shulman, 2004, p 175), arguing that teaching is an art, *[e]very art has rules but knowledge of the rules does not make one an artist. Art arises as the knower of rules learns to apply them appropriately to the particular case. Application, in turn, requires acute awareness of the particularities of that case and ways in which that rule can be modified to fit the case without complete abrogation of the rule.* Teachers with the least experience are likely, rightly, initially to follow relatively simple rules and only gradually to gain the self-assurance to depart from them – and know the situations when this is appropriate.

Expertise involves trust in intuition, informed by evidence from theory and experience of specific situations, as the basis of discernment and judgement rather than unthinking compliance. As Sternberg and Horvath (1995, p 12) suggest, expert teachers are proficient at 'working the system' to obtain needed services for their students, adding that *such practical ability or 'savvy' is a nontrivial component of teaching effectiveness.* So, they do not just comply with what they are told, but exercise autonomy based on their informed judgement. While they comply with the rules and expectations that really matter, such teachers are prepared to bend the rules when this is in the children's interests. This is not to say that teachers should not comply with some external expectations, but that, in relation to how to teach, they should have the confidence to decide the pedagogy most appropriate to the particular context and group of children. However, such judgement has to be informed by the collective experience of others, if it is not to be a matter of personal whim.

A primary classteacher with a high level of expertise works on several fronts at any one time, with multiple goals which will vary for different individuals and groups. Inevitably, primary classteachers will teach some subject areas and some children better than others, but their expertise involves meeting a broad range of goals, over time, creating an inclusive and potentiating learning environment, based on a wide range of teacher knowledge. This cannot be adequately judged on the basis of test results or the observation of a single lesson, especially when this is as part of an inspection or monitoring process; just as the architect is not judged only by the building's roof or the shape, but by the success of how well the whole building works in that context, for those who use it.

Pointers towards developing expertise

This book is about what primary classteachers' expertise entails, rather than how to develop it, which would require more detailed consideration. However, let me offer a few pointers from the preceding discussion.

A continuum of professional development

Teacher expertise is learned, mostly through a cycle of action, reflection, abstraction and planning, informed by research and experience, one's own and that of others; and has constantly to be updated, like that of a doctor or lawyer, however much some teachers seem to be 'naturals'. Sternberg and Horvath (1995, p 9) distinguish between teachers who are experienced and those who are experts, although they suggest (p 12) that the knowledge associated with expertise generally increases with experience.

Berliner (2004, pp 204–5) summarises Glaser's theory that the development of expertise involves a change of agency over time, through three stages:

» *externally supported*, where the novice learns primarily from others in a structured environment;

» *transitional*, where there is guided practice to enable more self-monitoring and self-regulation, adopting an apprenticeship approach;

» *self-regulatory,* where those developing expertise increasingly control their own learning environments, choose their own challenges and receive appropriate feedback.

You may be struck, as I am, by the similarity with how children's own learning is best enhanced.

Teaching a class of young children is enormously complicated, with the expertise to do so requiring many years to develop. To suggest that this is possible with a short period of training is ridiculous and reinforces the idea that teaching young children is just applied common sense. So, an initial teacher education course is only part of a continuum of professional development, a constant process, over time, a journey where the destination is never reached. To develop expertise, teachers require a commitment to, and a pathway for, continuing professional development and continuous learning.

Elliott et al. (2011, p 85) indicate that much professional knowledge is tacit, procedural and context specific, leading to appropriate action in unpredictable situations, and intricately bound up with one's own goals, circumstances, dispositions and personalities. They argue that it is acquired from the individual's experience within a given context rather than through a high degree of direct input from others, through instruction or external policies or prescriptions. Chapter 2 indicated that expertise is likely to develop at different rates, in different aspects of the role. So for teachers this entails the gradual accumulation of knowledge of how to understand, and respond to, a range of situations; and learning increasingly to trust in, but to be cautious of, one's own judgement.

Berliner (2001, p 477) writes *learning to teach … is primarily about learning to codify knowledge in order to draw on it again.* For the primary classteacher, the knowledge required is personal and interpersonal, recognising the complexity of the dynamics of, and relationships within and beyond, the classroom, as well as craft and subject related. The latter does not just involve subject knowledge, but pedagogical content knowledge – how material can best be presented to particular groups of children – cross-curricular links and the procedures and ways of working associated with different disciplines. The emphasis should be more on learning processes than on outcomes and on the 'ordinary' details of classroom interactions rather than anything out of the ordinary.

Ways of developing expertise

Developing expertise involves teachers gradually building greater and well-informed professional confidence in their own judgement, as opposed to Barber's (2005) view, which saw this as involving teachers moving from (what he saw as) uninformed towards informed autonomy, by means of first uninformed and then informed prescription. Telling teachers how to teach and then expecting them to develop confidence in their own judgement overlooks how they have to draw on a wealth of lived experience to learn how best to respond to the unpredictability of the classroom.

Ideally, developing expertise is a collective as well as an individual process, where individuals can draw on the wisdom of others, from research and the practice of those with greater experience. This is maybe more like learning to be a parent than we might imagine; or to drive, which I found frustratingly difficult. Nothing can quite prepare one, though theory and preparation can help. So, the parent learns through being a parent, in many respects having to trust intuition, but guided by the experience of others, especially those who understand the challenges and possibilities in that particular situation. And the driver starts with simple rules, but finds that only in applying them does the whole process start to make sense.

A key way for teachers to develop their own expertise is to recognise, and to grapple, both individually and with other colleagues, with the complexities of individual children's backgrounds, culture, ethnicity, and class, and of the emotional and social dynamics of the classroom, and how these affect children's learning. And so to think of, and try out, possible patterns of resolution appropriate to particular individuals, groups and classes, rather than just to follow the script.

Teachers benefit from watching other teachers at work, or working alongside them, looking to identify and discuss dilemmas and successful patterns of resolution rather than concentrating on shortcomings. Yet, after qualification, teachers work most of the time largely on their own, little supported in the actual task of teaching – unlike a junior doctor or an architect. And they are rarely watched at work by other adults, and then usually in the context of being monitored, to ensure compliance with external demands. While this may be necessary for some purposes, it should not be confused with professional development to develop expertise, where alternative strategies can be explored in a non-judgemental way. Monitoring may help to establish whether a teacher is adequate, but it is a poor strategy to develop expertise.

Experts recognise the limits of their expertise and are prepared to call on others, where need be. In teaching, this involves drawing on the expertise of other people, both within and beyond the school, and sharing their own. This is much easier in a school context where others provide support. Just as the learning environment influences profoundly how children learn, the school and policy environment affects how teachers are encouraged, or otherwise, to exercise and develop their expertise. This requires headteachers and colleagues who encourage each other to explore, to risk, to innovate – and support each other through the successes and the difficulties.

Shulman highlights the value of case studies in developing professional expertise, suggesting (2004, p 564) that these are valuable because *participants are urged to elaborate on … what actually happened, what was said and done, how all that occurred made them feel … to dig deep into the particularity of the context because it is in the devilish details that practice differs dramatically from theory.* Given the difficulty of groups of teachers watching actual lessons, scenarios and videos of real-life dilemmas, rather than exemplary lessons, seem the best way, practically, of encouraging reflection and discussion about these.

Watching and discussing with others with a high level of expertise is a necessary part of teachers developing expertise. But it is not enough. Underlying how teachers act is how they think. So teachers have to challenge – and often try to change – how they think about ideas such as intelligence and inclusion, behaviour and breadth, curriculum and challenge. For instance, Twiselton's (2006) research into primary student teachers characterises some as 'task managers', with little emphasis on children's learning, some as 'curriculum deliverers', where the focus is more on learning but largely based on external demands, and some as 'concept/skill builders', where they understand and encourage patterns of learning beyond the task. If teachers are to see themselves as curriculum creators rather than deliverers, initial teacher education must at least open up this possibility; and continuing professional development must encourage it.

FINAL **THOUGHTS**

Chapter 1 started with the quotation from Shulman that doctors would hardly ever be faced with a situation of comparable complexity to that of the classteacher. Yet, teachers are expected to do so every day. The quotation at the start of this chapter emphasised the key role of teachers, not just as technicians but as people whose view of life is deeply influential. So, we face a remarkable paradox. Primary classteachers fulfil a complex role with a profound impact on children. Yet their status is lower than that of otherwise comparable professions, and even other teachers, the confidence of many is low and there is pressure to focus on a narrow range of goals and measurable outcomes.

A profession able to develop the knowledge, dispositions and values for children to thrive in a complex and changing society requires teachers with a greater belief in their expertise and judgement. It is hard to see the answer coming from policy-makers or politicians. So it is long overdue that teachers of young children receive the status the role deserves; but to gain this they, and those who support them in their practice and through research, must recognise and articulate both to each other and more widely what the classteacher's role really entails and how those with a high level of expertise fulfil it.

REFERENCES

Alexander, R.J. (1992) *Policy and Practice in Primary Education*. London: Routledge.

Alexander, R.J. (1995) *Versions of Primary Education*. London: Methuen.

Alexander, R.J. (2000) *Culture and Pedagogy: International Comparisons in Primary Education*. Oxford: Blackwell.

Alexander, R.J. (2004) Still No Pedagogy? Principle, Pragmatism and Compliance in Primary Education. *Cambridge Journal of Education*, 34(1): 7–33.

Alexander, R.J. (ed) (2010) *Children, Their World, Their Education – Final Report and Recommendations of the Cambridge Primary Review*. Abingdon: Routledge.

Barber, M. (2005) *Informed Professionalism: Realising the Potential*. London, Presentation to a Conference of the Association of Teachers and Lecturers.

Berlak, A. and Berlak, H. (1981) *Dilemmas of Schooling: Teaching and Social Change*. London: Methuen.

Berliner, D.C. (2001) Learning about and Learning from Expert Teachers. *International Journal of Educational Research*, 35: 463–82.

Berliner, D.C. (2004) Describing the Behavior and Documenting the Accomplishments of Expert Teachers. *Bulletin of Science, Technology and Society*, 24(3): 200–12.

Black, P. (1999) Assessment, Learning Theories and Testing Systems, in Murphy, P. (ed) *Learners, Learning and Assessment* (pp 118–34). London: Paul Chapman Publishing.

Black, P. and Wiliam, D. (1998) *Inside the Black Box – Raising Standards through Classroom Assessment*. London: Kings' College School of Education.

Black, P., Harrison, C., Lee, C., Marshall, B. and Wiliam, D. (2002) *Working inside the Black Box: Assessment for Learning in the Classroom*. London: Kings' College School of Education.

Bone, J. (2010) Spirituality and Early Childhood Education: 'Belonging, Being and Becoming' at a Midwinter Festival. *Journal of Religious Education*, 58(3): 26–34.

Brantlinger, E. (2003) *Dividing Classes: How the Middle Class Negotiates and Rationalizes School Advantage*. London: RoutledgeFalmer.

Brown, J.S., Collins, A. and Duguid, P. (1989) Situated Cognition and the Culture of Learning. *Educational Researcher*, 18(1): 32–42.

Bruner, J.S. (1960) *The Process of Education*. Cambridge (Mass.): Harvard University Press.

Bruner, J.S. (1996) *The Culture of Education*. Cambridge (Mass.): Harvard University Press.

Bruner, J.S. (2006) *In Search of Pedagogy: The Selected Works of Jerome S. Bruner* (2 volumes). Abingdon: Routledge.

Claxton, G. (1997) *Hare Brain, Tortoise Mind – Why Intelligence Increases When You Think Less*. London: Fourth Estate.

Claxton, G. (2002) *Building Learning Power: Helping Young People Become Better Learners*. Bristol: TLO Ltd.

Claxton, G. (2007) Expanding Young People's Capacity to Learn. *British Journal of Educational Studies*, 55(2): 115–34.

Claxton, G. and Carr, M. (2004) A Framework for Teaching Learning: The Dynamics of Disposition. *Early Years*, 24(1): 87–97.

Cooper, P. and McIntyre, D. (1996) *Effective Teaching and Learning: Teachers' and Students' Perspectives*. Buckingham: Open University Press.

Department for Education (DfE) (2012) *Teachers' Standards*. www.education.gov.uk/schools/leadership/deployingstaff/a00205581/teachers-standards1-sep-2012, accessed 24 September 2012.

Desforges, C. (1995) *An Introduction to Teaching: psychological perspectives*. Oxford: Blackwell.

Donaldson, M. (1982) *Children's Minds*. Glasgow: Fontana.

Donaldson, M. (1992) *Human Minds – An Exploration*. London: Allen Lane.

Dweck, C.S. (2000) *Self Theories: Their Role in Motivation, Personality and Development*. Philadelphia: Psychology Press.

Eaude, T. (2008) *Children's Spiritual, Moral, Social and Cultural Development – Primary and Early Years*. Exeter: Learning Matters.

Eaude, T. (2011) *Thinking through Pedagogy for Primary and Early Years*. Exeter: Learning Matters.

Eraut, M. (2000) The Intuitive Practitioner – a Critical Overview, in Atkinson, T. and Claxton, G. (eds) *The Intuitive Practitioner – on the Value of Not Always Knowing What One Is Doing* (pp 255–68). Buckingham: Open University Press.

Ericsson, K.A. and Smith, J. (1991) *Toward a General Theory of Expertise: Prospects and Limits*. Cambridge: Cambridge University Press.

Elliott, J.G., Stemler, S.E., Sternberg, R.J., Grigorenko, E.L. and Hoffman, N. (2011) The Socially Skilled Teacher and the Development of Tacit Knowledge. *British Educational Research Journal*, 37(1): 83–103.

Fullan, M. (1991) *The New Meaning of Educational Change*. London: Cassell.

Galton, M., Simon, B. and Croll, P. (1980) *Inside the Primary Classroom*. London: Routledge, Kegan and Paul.

Galton, M., Hargreaves, L., Comber, C., Wall, D. and Pell, A. (1999) *Inside the Primary Classroom: 20 Years on*. London: Routledge.

Gardner, H. (1993) *The Unschooled Mind – How Children Think and How Schools Should Teach*. London: Fontana.

Gerhardt, S. (2004) *Why Love Matters: How Affection Shapes a Baby's Brain*. Hove: Routledge.

Glaser, R. (1999) Expert Knowledge and Processes of Thinking, in McCormick, R. and Paechter, C. (eds) *Learning and Knowledge* (pp 88–102). London: Paul Chapman Publishing.

Grimmett, P.P. and Mackinnon, A.M. (1992) Craft Knowledge and the Education of Teachers. *Review of Research in Education*, 18: 385–456.

Hart, S., Dixon, A., Drummond, M.J. and McIntyre, D. (2004) *Learning without Limits*. Maidenhead: Open University Press.

Ireson, J., Mortimore, P. and Hallam, S. (1999) The Common Strands of Pedagogy and Their Implications, in Mortimore, P. (ed) *Understanding Pedagogy and Its Impact on Learning* (pp 212–32). London: Paul Chapman Publishing.

Jackson, P.W. (1968) *Life in Classrooms*. New York: Holt, Rinehart and Winston.

Jackson, P.W., Boostrom R.E, and Hansen D.J. (1993) *The Moral Life of Schools*. San Francisco: Jossey Bass.

John, P. (2000) Awareness and Intuition: How Student Teachers Read Their Own Lessons, in Atkinson, T. and Claxton, G. (eds) *The Intuitive Practitioner – on the Value of Not Always Knowing What One Is Doing* (pp 84–106). Buckingham: Open University Press.

John, P. (2008) The Predicament of the Teaching Profession and the Revival of Professional Authority: A Parsonian Perspective, in Johnson, D. and Maclean, R. (eds) *Teaching: Professionalization, Development and Leadership* (pp 11–24). Springer, www.springer.com.

Katz, L. (2003) Current Issues and Trends in Early Childhood Education, in Saraswathi, T.S. (ed) *Cross Cultural Perspectives in Human Development: Theory, Research and Application* (pp 354–82). London: Sage.

Kimes Myers, B. (1997) *Young Children and Spirituality*. London: Routledge.

Lave, J. (1988) *Cognition in Practice: Mind, Mathematics and Culture in Everyday Life*. Cambridge: Cambridge University Press.

Mayall, B. (2010) Children's Lives outside School and Their Educational Impact, in Alexander, R. (ed) *The Cambridge Primary Review Research Surveys* (pp 49–82). Abingdon: Routledge.

McEwan, I. (1997) *Enduring Love*. London: Jonathan Cape.

Nias, J. (1989) *Primary Teachers Talking: A Study of Teaching as Work*. London: Routledge.

Noddings, N. (2003) *Caring – a Feminine Approach to Ethics and Moral Education*. Berkeley: University of California Press.

Nussbaum, M. (2010) *Not for Profit: Why Democracy Needs the Humanities*. Princeton: Princeton University Press.

Ofsted (2010) *Learning: Creative Approaches that Raise Standards* via www.ofsted.gov.uk/Ofsted-home/Publications-and-research, accessed 30 September 2012.

Palmer, P.J. (1983, 1993) *To Know as We Are Known. Education as a Spiritual Journey*. San Francisco: HarperSanFrancisco.

Papert, S. (1999) www.papert.org/articles/Papertonpiaget.html, accessed 24 September 2012.

Polanyi, M. (1967) *The Tacit Dimension*. London: Routledge.

Pollard, A. (1985) *The Social World of the Primary School*. London: Holt, Rinehart and Winston.

Pollard, A. (ed) (2010) *Professionalism and Pedagogy: A Contemporary Opportunity. A Commentary by TLRP and GTCE*. London: TLRP.

Rogoff, B. (1990) *Apprenticeship in Thinking – Cognitive Development in Social Context*. Oxford: Oxford University Press.

Ruthven, K., Hennessey, S. and Deaney, R. (2004) *Eliciting Situated Expertise in ICT-Integrated Mathematics and Science Teaching*. University of Cambridge/ ESRC via www.educ.cam.ac.uk/research/projects/istl/Set-itFullReport.pdf.

Salzberger-Wittenberg, I., Henry, G. and Osborne, E. (1983) *The Emotional Experience of Learning and Teaching*. London: Routledge and Kegan Paul.

Sawyer, R.K. (2004) Creative Teaching: Collaborative Discussion as Disciplined Improvisation. *Educational Researcher*, 33(2): 12–20.

Schemp, P.G., Manross, D., Tan, S.K.S. and Fincher, M.D. (1998) Subject Expertise and Teachers' Knowledge. *Journal of Teaching Physical Education*, 17: 342–56.

Schon, D. (1987) *Educating the Reflective Practitioner: Toward a New Design for Teaching and Learning the Professions*. San Francisco: Jossey Bass.

Shulman, L.S. (2004) *The Wisdom of Practice – Essays on Teaching, Learning and Learning to Teach*. San Francisco: Jossey Bass.

Simon, B. (1981) Why No Pedagogy in England?, in Simon, B. and Taylor, W. (eds) *Education in The Eighties: The Central Issues* (pp 124–45). London: Batsford.

Sternberg, R.J. and Horvath, J.A. (1995) A Prototype View of Expert Teaching. *Educational Researcher*, 24(6): 9–17.

Swann, M., Peacock, A., Hart, S. and Drummond, M.J. (2012) *Creating Learning without Limits*. Maidenhead: Open University Press.

TLRP (Teaching and Learning Research Programme) (2006) *Improving Teaching and Learning in Schools*. London: TLRP (see www.tlrp.org).

Troman, G. (1996) Models of the 'Good' Teacher: Defining and Redefining Teacher Quality, in Woods, P. (ed) *Contemporary Issues in Teaching and Learning* (pp 20–37). London: Routledge.

Turner-Bissett, R. (1999) The Knowledge Bases of the Expert Teacher. *British Educational Research Journal*, 25(1): 39–55.

Turner-Bissett, R. (2001) *Expert Teaching: Knowledge and Pedagogy to Lead the Profession*. London: David Fulton.

Twiselton, S. (2006) The Problem with English: The Exploration and Development of Student Teachers' English Subject Knowledge in Primary Classrooms. *Literacy*, 40(2): 88–96.

Vygotsky, L.S. (1978) *Mind in Society: The Development of Higher Mental Processes*. Cambridge (Mass.): Harvard University Press.

Wynne, B. (1991) Knowledges in Context. *Science, Technology and Human Values*, 16(1): 111–21.

INDEX

A

ability, in theory, 12, 21, 62
adaptability, 22, 23, 49–50, 58–59
Alexander, R.J., 3, 18, 20, 26, 37, 38, 41, 52
anxiety, child, 33, 35
apprenticeship approach to teaching, 52–54,
    see also example, learning by
assessment
    children's learning, 22–23, 40, 47
    of expertise, 8, 15, 17–18, 59
attitudes and beliefs, teacher, 18–19, 27–28, 55, 62
automaticity, 13
autonomy, 39, 59

B

Barber, M., 61
beliefs, teacher, 18–19, 27–28, 55, 62
Bereiter, C., 12
Berlak, A., 25
Berlak, H., 25
Berliner, D.C., 7–8, 12, 18, 22, 39, 60, 61
bi-directionality, 39
Black, P., 34, 46, 47
Bond, L., 19, 27
Bone, J., 32
Brantlinger, E., 38
Bruner, J.S., 23, 33, 34

C

Cambridge Primary Review, 2, 3, 40, 58
caring, 35
Carr, M., 36–37
change, learning to cope with, 48, 55
children
    funds of knowledge, 27–28
    learning, 32–37, 50, 52
    monitoring, 22
    mutual support and feedback, 49
    setting objectives, 48
class discussions, 50
classroom adults, 41
classroom dynamics, 38–39
classteachers, primary
    12 propositions on expertise, 56
    beyond the classroom, 41–42
    compared to medical practitioners, 10
    continuity of, 45, 46
    role, 31–32
Claxton, G., 36–37, 48, 53
cognition, emotional link, 33
collective responsibility, 10
competition, 38–39
confident uncertainty, 53
context, link with expertise, 8, 15, 60

continuing professional development, 60–61, 62
control, 26, 41, 52
Cooper, P., 17, 33, 39
craft knowledge, 21–22, *see also* pedagogical
    content knowledge (PCK)
crystallised expertise, 12
cues, pupil, interpretation of, 24, 49–50
cultural capital, 27
culture of compliance, 2, 40
culture, link to expertise, 18
curriculum
    breadth, 37
    detail, 40

D

decisiveness, 13
Desforges, C., 52
didactic teaching, 52
dilemmas, 25–26, 45
disciplined improvisation, 23
disposition to learn, 52
diversity, 24, 26–27, 51
domain knowledge, 21, *see also* pedagogical
    content knowledge (PCK)
Donaldson, M., 33
Dweck, C.S., 28, 49

E

Eaude, T., 27, 31, 55
Education Act (2011), 31
education aims, 31–32
Elliott, J.G., 21, 60
empathy, 35
England, pedagogical tradition, 3
enthusiasm, 54
environment, learning, 24, 36–37, 51
Eraut, M., 23
Erikson, E., 39
example, learning by, 35–36
expectations
    external, 14–15, 39, 59
    of children, 27
experience, 10, 11, 59, 60
expertise
    12 propositions about classteachers, 56
    assessment, 8, 15, 17–18, 59
    context, 8, 15, 60
    culture, link to, 18
    development, 9–10, 60–62
    difficulties describing, 7–9, 17
    external, 47
    fluid, 12–14, 22–24, 58–59
    key areas, 19–20
    prototypical nature, 12, 15
    stages of, 58–59